This book belongs to

Dauid Barry
Cowmeadow.
Christmas 86.

Practical & Decorative Woodworking Joints

Practical & Decorative Woodworking Joints

John E. N. Bairstow

B.T. Batsford Ltd, London

First published 1984
© John E.N. Bairstow 1984

ISBN 0 7134 4211 5 (cased)

Typeset by Tek-Art Ltd, Kent
and printed in Great Britain by
Butler & Tanner Ltd
Frome, Somerset
for the publishers
B.T. Batsford Ltd
4 Fitzhardinge Street
London W1H 0AH

Contents

Acknowledgements

The author would also like to thank the following for permission to photograph items in their collections: Miss J.N. Muncey (colour plates 1 and 3); Mr and Mrs L. Ellis (colour plate 7).

My grateful thanks are due first to the Winston Churchill Memorial Trust for assisting me to undertake valuable research in the U.S.A.; to Mr W.A.W. Elloway for continued support in the development of my work; to John Harlow Ott and June Sprigg of Hancock Shaker Village, Brother Theodore Johnson and family of Sabbathday Lake, Mr Randell L. Makinson, Mr Robert H. Ellsworth, Wendell Castle and Stephen Proctor for various parts of my research. Finally to Miss Gillian Bairstow, Mr Brian Mee and Mr Robert Cox for assistance in completing the book.

Introduction

Ever since the earliest days of timber being used as a constructional material, some method of connecting the components has been sought. Many types of joint have been developed, varying greatly in their complexity, and it is to the woodworker's advantage to have a firm grasp of the principles behind their creation.

The development of the functional aspect of the joint has been extensive, with various forms of the dovetail and mortise and tenon being the mainstay of wooden construction for centuries. However, although it has always been the tendency to apply decoration to a piece of furniture – such as carving, inlay or marquetry – the decorative potential of the joint has remained relatively undeveloped. Examples of standard and decorative joinery are illustrated in this book in an attempt to show the many variations available to anyone working in wood.

Although a limited number of exposed joints have always been used, they became increasingly less popular with the introduction of machinery into furniture manufacture which made it cheaper to produce simple, 'secret' joinery. An additional problem is that most standard types of joint, such as the dovetail, rarely relate to the form of a piece of furniture because they concentrate all the interest along the corners. This is fine if it is being closely inspected but, when viewed from more than a few feet away, the beauty of detail is lost and the most striking thing is the overall form.

In selecting timbers for constructing a decorative joint, two points must be considered if it is to be successful. The development of modern adhesives allows far more enterprising configurations to be made where the glue line is often stronger than the timber. However, this must not conflict with the nature of wood, or weakness could ensue. In addition, contrasting timbers should have similar qualities to prevent undue contrasts in rates of expansion and contraction.

Wooden structures are usually built in either the frame or the carcase, each having its own types of joint. Both areas are studied, with various decorative possibilities being discussed and illustrated. The splicing joint, while no longer an essential form of construction due to modern adhesives, is important because it shows what can be achieved when new forms are considered, and will be of interest to the woodworker because of its complexity.

The process of cutting any joint is variable and depends on the maker's preferences. All the following joints, other than my own designs, are a personal interpretation which have been found to work effectively in their chosen situation.

1 Preparation and Working Methods

If any joint is to be made to a high standard, then each component must be prepared accurately to length, width and thickness. After checking the timber carefully for defects, initial cutting should allow an additional 1.2cm (½in.) in the length and 6mm (¼in.) on the width of finished sizes. Depending on the size of timber being used, an allowance of 3mm (⅛in.) is usually allowed for planing to thickness. Large boards may require more than this if sticking or cutting to thickness has been badly executed.

Initially, the face side is planed flat using the jack plane and working with the grain to prevent tearing (*diagram 1*). When working with wide boards, planing diagonally or across the grain, particularly if it is interlocking, will yield better results. The surface should be checked continually with a straight edge for flatness and with winding strips for twist. If the board is twisted the winding strips will help to show it (*diagram 2*), and efforts should be made to correct it

direction of planing

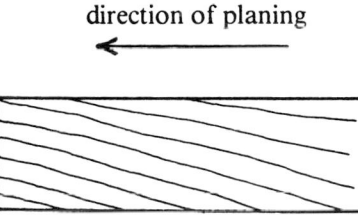

Diagram 1 *Planing should follow the same direction as the grain to prevent the tearing of timber fibres*

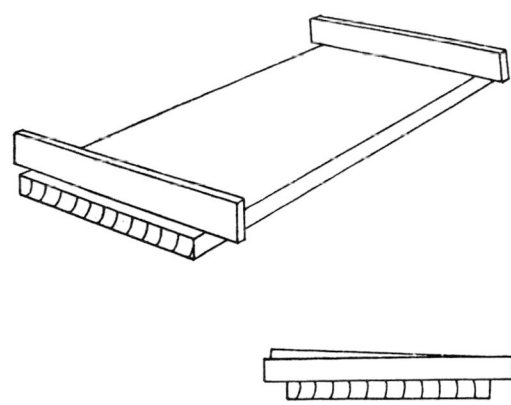

by removing timber at the high points until flatness is achieved (*diagram 3*). Any roughness or rippling is removed by taking fine shavings, initially with the try-plane and finishing with the smoothing plane, to give a good clean

Diagram 2 *Winding strips help to show if a board is twisted.*

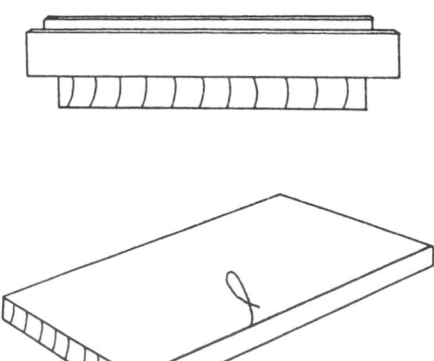

Diagram 3 *Parallel winding strips indicate that twist has been removed.*

Diagram 4 *A simple, looped pencil line indicates the face side.*

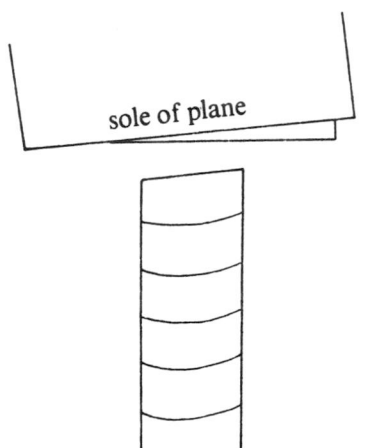

sole of plane

Diagram 5 *Lateral adjustment of the plane blade helps correct a bevelled edge.*

Diagram 6 *The face edge is marked as indicated when it is straight and perpendicular to the face side.*

surface. This can then be marked as the face side (*diagram 4*).

The face edge, which is straight in its length and square to the face side, is planed true with the try-plane. Although achieving a straight edge is relatively simple, difficulty may be experienced when attempting to make it square with the face side, the usual result being a bevel. This should be corrected by adjusting the blade laterally to compensate for the angle (*diagram 5*), removing more timber at the high point. The ability to tilt the sole of the plane to correct the bevel requires experience in tool use and should not be attempted by beginners. When this edge is correct it can be marked as the face edge (*diagram 6*). The importance of an accurate face side and face edge cannot be over-stressed if marking out of the joint is to be accurate, as all lines stem from these surfaces.

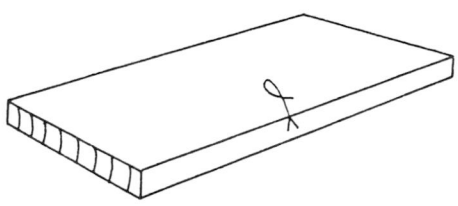

The required thickness is determined by gauging around the edges with a marking gauge and planing down to these lines with a try-plane (*diagram 7*). There is usually a tendency to remove waste at the edges more quickly than at the middle of the board and this should be avoided by continual checking with a straight edge.

The finished width of the board is scribed from the face

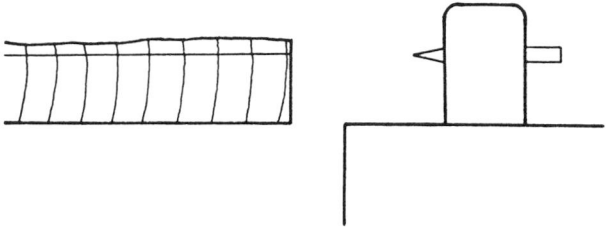

Diagram 7 *The marking gauge scribes in the board thickness.*

edge on both surfaces using the marking gauge (*diagram 8*). The waste is removed with the try-plane to give a parallel edged board.

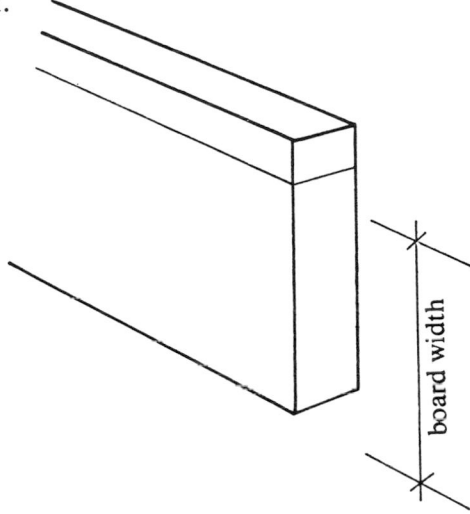

board width

Diagram 8 *The board width is scribed with the marking gauge from the face edge.*

The length of the timber is determined by squaring round each end with the knife and try-square. In most exposed joinery the length is usually increased by adding 1.5mm (¹/₁₆in.) at each end for planing back to the surface after construction. If the timber is small enough to allow easy handling, a shooting board is used to remove the waste (*diagram 9*). Alternatively, the timber is placed in the vice,

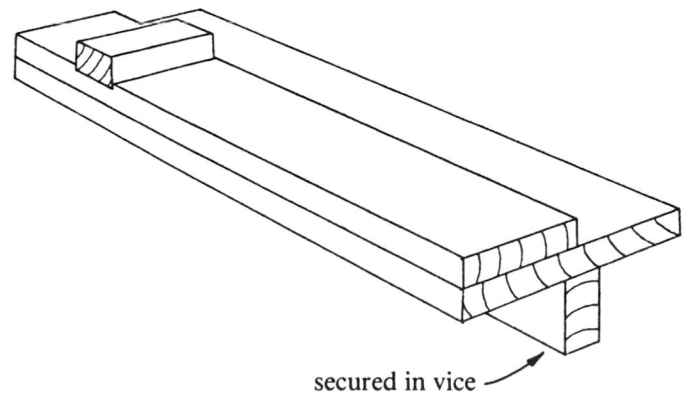

secured in vice

Diagram 9 *The shooting board, used to plane square the end grain of a component.*

Diagram 10 *The waste at one corner should be removed before attempting to plane across the full width of a board.*

and waste removed by working in both directions with the try-plane (*diagram 10*). This will prevent the timber splitting, which would occur if an attempt were made to remove waste from one direction only (*diagram 11*). The

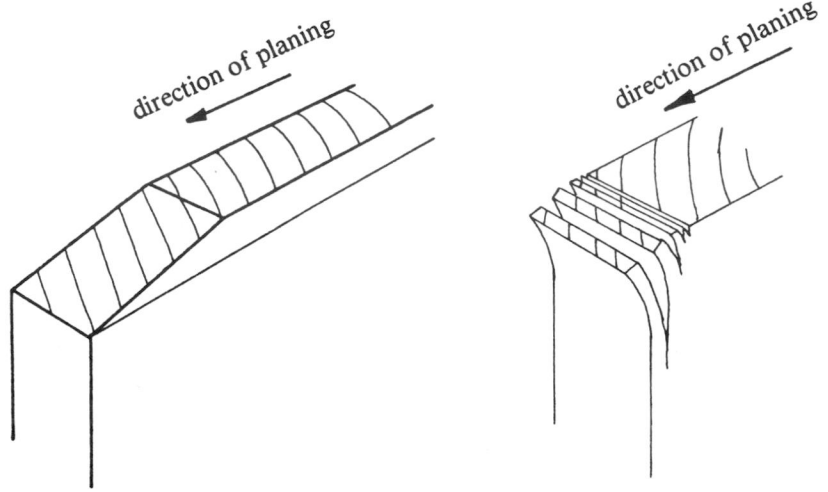

Diagram 11 *The end grain will split if an attempt is made to plane beyond it.*

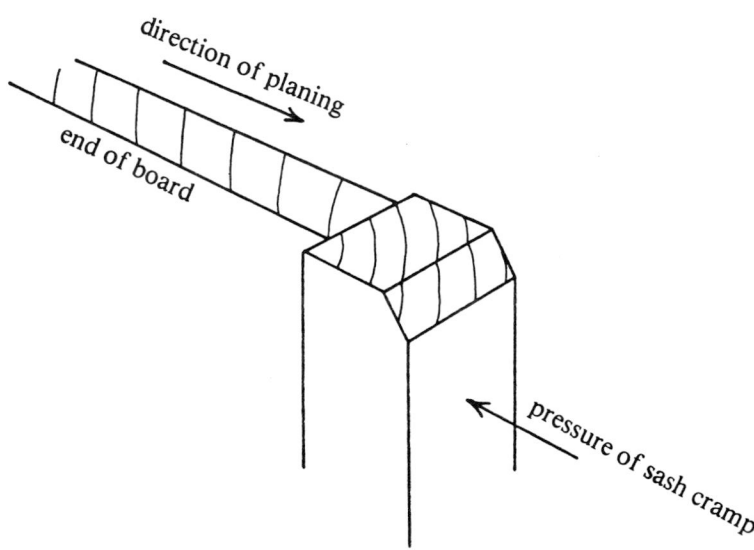

Diagram 12 *Waste material supports the timber to prevent splitting.*

timber can be worked in one direction if a piece of waste material is cramped to the end (*diagram 12*).

If this procedure is followed, the timber will be ready for jointing. It should, however, be stacked between stickers (*diagram 13*) when not in use to help prevent any sort of movement, such as twisting or cupping.

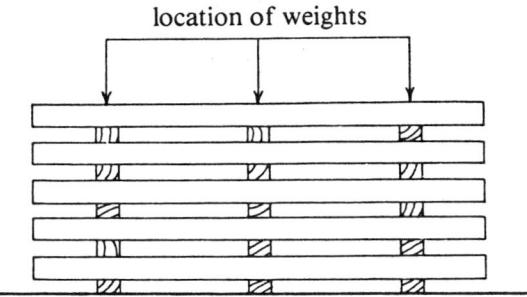

location of weights

Diagram 13 *Stacking timber between stickers allows air to circulate, thus preventing undue drying out as well as minimizing any tendency to warp or cup.*

MARKING OUT

Precise, distinct marking out lines will greatly assist in the accurate cutting of any joint. Generally, all lines in a joint that run across the grain or are trimmed with a chisel (such as at the inside shoulder) should be marked with a knife, usually with the aid of a try-square or sliding bevel. Using a single-bevelled knife, press the try-square into position,

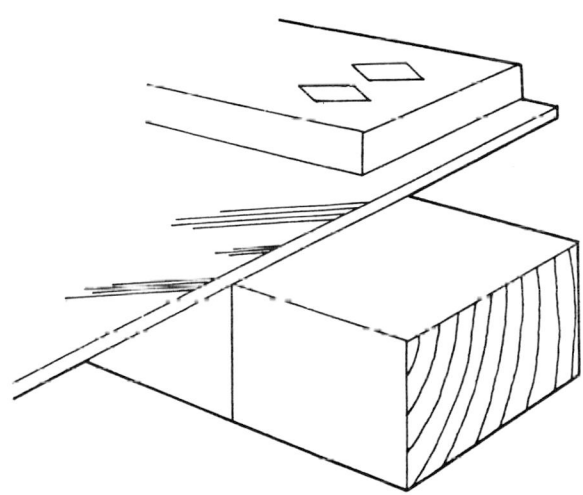

Diagram 14 *Always place the try-square blade on the timber that will be retained.*

resting on the part of the timber that will be retained (*diagram 14*) and cut in the line. On the side nearest the square the line will be clean and sharp, while the other side will be slightly bevelled (*diagram 15*). Although this may seem a minor point, every effort should be made to produce a well-fitting joint. If opposite joints have the same inside shoulder, the two components can be cramped together and marked, giving identical lengths.

All lines that run parallel to the face side or face edge, such as the outline of a tenon, are scribed with the marking gauge or mortise gauge. There are, of course, exceptions to this,

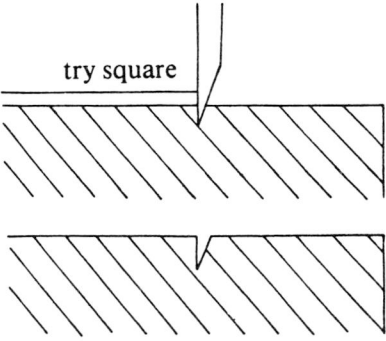

try square

Diagram 15 *The knife cut will be square at one side and slightly bevelled on the other.*

13

such as marking in the finger joint which is treated like the dovetail joint. This should always be carried out with a sharp H pencil to give a positive, easy-to-read line. For such accurate work, never use a soft lead as this gives an inaccurate reading, or a hard lead, which may not show up significantly.

The mitre is an important feature in many of the joints to be discussed and has to be set out accurately for it to be efficient. The commercially available mitre square is rarely set at precisely 45° and, although it is usually only slightly out of true, will cause considerable error if used on all four corners of a carcase, which will multiply the inaccuracy four times.

To achieve the precise angle use the sliding bevel which is infinitely variable and therefore easily set. To set it, first test a try-square for 90° by holding its stock against a straight edge and drawing in the right angle. Reverse the square and re-align the blade with the pencil line. This should be the same if the square is a true right angle (*diagram 16*). Plane a

Diagram 16 *Parallel lines indicate a true right angle while any deviation shows the try-square to be at fault.*

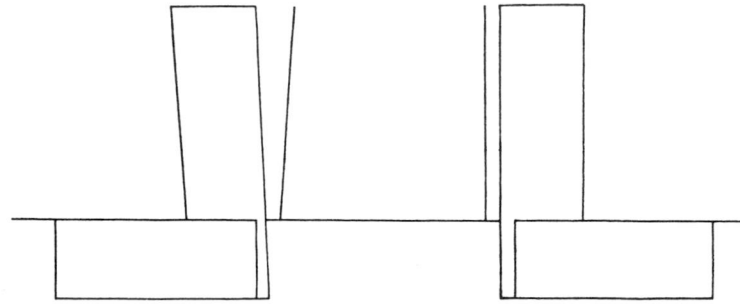

square corner on a piece of plywood and test it for accuracy with the try-square. When this is true, set the sliding bevel to about 45°, press the stock against one edge of the corner and draw in the angle using a sharp pencil. Set the stock on the adjacent edge and line up the blade with the pencil line. Only when the two readings give the same line will the angle on the sliding bevel be at exactly 45°.

CUTTING
This is usually done with a tenon or dovetail saw, depending on the size of the joint to be cut. To start the cut off accurately, use a few teeth at the front of the saw on the corner of the timber with the blade held at 45° (*diagram 17*). As the cut gets deeper, gradually use more of the blade and bring it into the horizontal position. The cut is then made in this position down to the shoulder line.

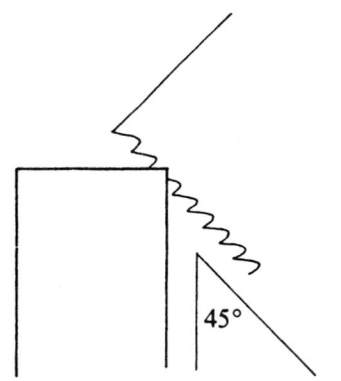

Diagram 17 *Start a sawcut by using the front few teeth of a blade held at 45°.*

FITTING

Invariably, there will be the occasion when a joint is cut that is too tight a fit and requires further removal of waste. If this is done at the wrong point then a gap in the finished joint may result, and so some knowledge of where to trim the timber is essential. To test for fit, the joint will have been lightly tapped together, but tightness in certain areas will prevent its assembly. Take the joint apart and look at the meeting faces of the joint for any areas that shine when held up to the light. Over-tightness of the joint will cause compression of the fibres which will show as a reflective surface. Such areas should be lightly trimmed before attempting to put the joint together again.

GLUING

When gluing a joint together with either C-cramp or sash cramp, some form of block will be needed between the metal and the timber to prevent any sort of bruising occuring while applying pressure where it is needed. The dovetail or finger joint requires specially prepared blocks to exert pressure on

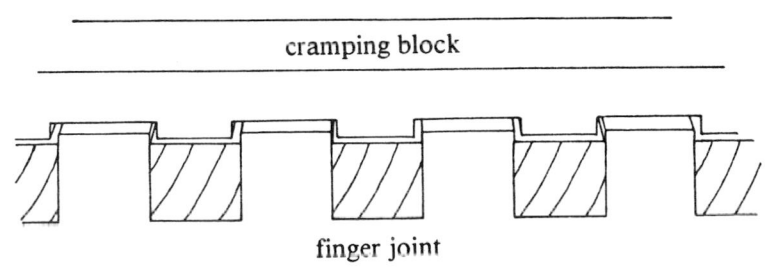

Diagram 18 *Cramping blocks are shaped to provide pressure only where it is needed.*

the tail or finger while spanning the protrusions of the adjoining panel (*diagram 18*). The block can be slightly curved so that, when the cramps are tightened on the outsides, initial pressure is exerted in the centre (*diagram 19*).

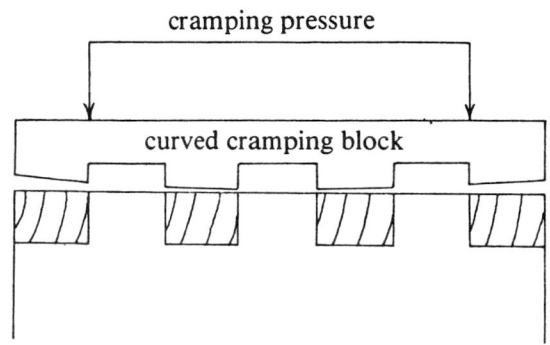

Diagram 19 *Curved cramping blocks provide pressure at the centre when cramped on the outsides.*

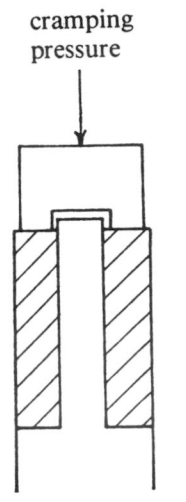

cramping
pressure

Diagram 20 *The cramping block used on the through mortise and tenon is shaped to span the protrusion.*

Other through joints, such as the mortise and tenon, are treated in a similar way, the blocks being shaped to span any protrusion (*diagram 20*).

Conventional methods of gluing together a mitred frame or carcase are usually difficult because of the number of cramps needed to run across all corners. This can be overcome by gluing a triangular block on to the timber so that one of its sides is parallel to the face of the mitre (*diagram 21*). Adjacent panels are then glued together by exerting pressure with C-cramps across the blocks (*diagram 22*). This method allows fine adjustment of each mitre without upsetting any other corner, which is what usually happens when using the sash-cramp. The blocks are easily removed by sawing and planing once the joint is secure.

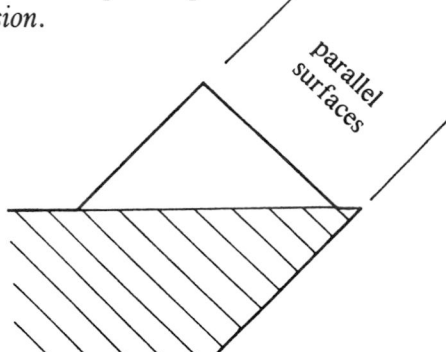

parallel surfaces

Diagram 21 *A triangular block glued to the board should have one face parallel to the mitre.*

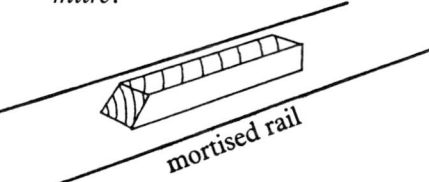

mortised rail

Diagram 23 *The end grain of any protrusion is prevented from splitting by removing the inside corner with a chisel and planing towards it.*

Diagram 24 *The front of the plane is pressed on the adjacent panel or rail while cuts are made to remove the waste.*

pressure of C-cramp

Diagram 22 *Adjacent boards are joined by applying pressure on the triangular blocks with C-cramps.*

Finishing

When a joint has been glued together, there should be some protrusion of waste timber that has to be removed in order to finish off the construction and this is done by planing across the end grain. In order to prevent this splitting, remove the inside corners of the waste and plane towards this (*diagram 23*). Press the front of the plane on the adjacent panel or rail (*diagram 24*) and make cuts until the sole is gradually worked into the horizontal position.

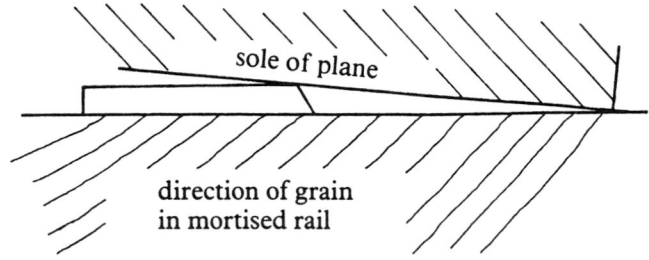

sole of plane

direction of grain
in mortised rail

2 Framing Joints

MORTISE AND TENON

The basis for many joints used in framework is the mortise and tenon and it is an essential starting point in the development of wooden construction. It forms the foundation of many of the decorative and practical joints under discussion in this chapter.

Basic mortise and tenon

The variations of mortise and tenon are used to connect two pieces of timber most commonly at a right angle. In its basic form, the joint is used to connect a rail to a leg using a stopped mortise and stub tenon (*diagram 25*).

Initial marking out of the leg gives the mortise a length that is approximately 6mm (¼in.) shorter than the width of the connecting rail. Set the mortise gauge to approximately one-third of the rail thickness, in fact to the nearest available mortise chisel. The parallel lines are then scribed between the extremities of the mortise (*diagram 26*). Its depth is about three-quarters the thickness of the leg.

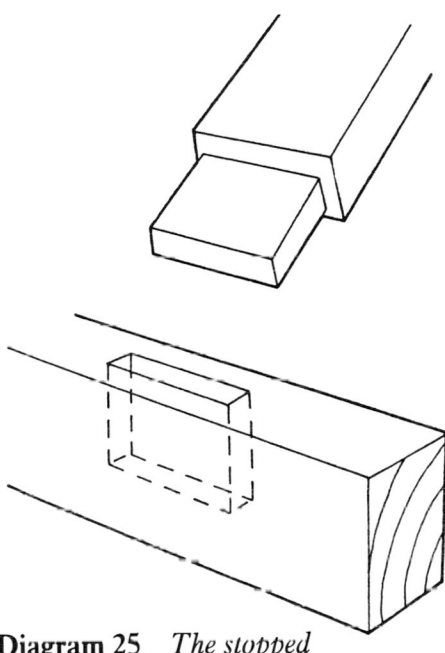

Diagram 25 *The stopped mortise and stub tenon.*

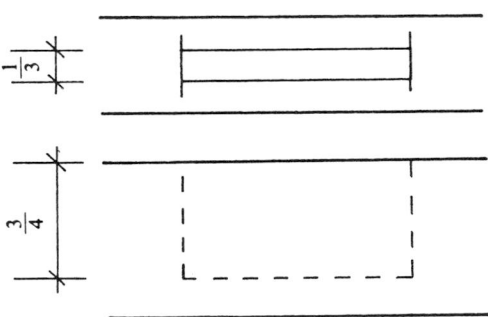

Diagram 26 *The outline of the mortise.*

The length of the tenon is slightly shorter than the depth of the mortise, measured from the end of the rail and marked in with the aid of a knife and try-square. A small gap at the

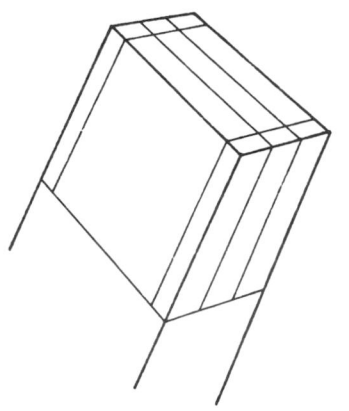

Diagram 27 *The outline of the tenon, marked with the mortise and marking gauges.*

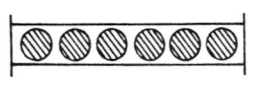

Diagram 28 *Waste is removed with a brace and bit. The bit should be slightly smaller than the mortise width.*

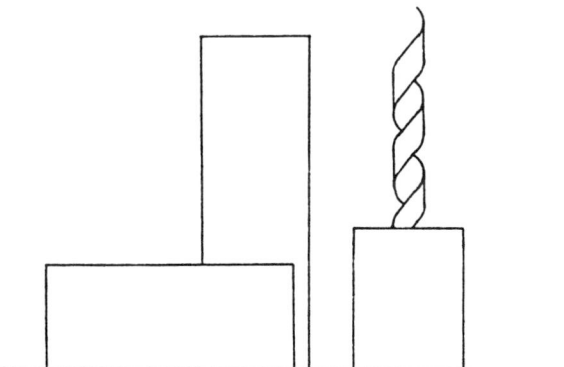

Diagram 29 *When removing the mortise waste, view the bit from the end of the timber to ensure a cut that is parallel to the face side.*

bottom of the mortise will be produced, because of the difference in length, which will take up any excess glue and so alleviate unnecessary pressure. The mortise gauge is used at the same setting to mark in the thickness of the tenon and a marking gauge set at 3mm (⅛in.) scribes the shoulder from each edge (*diagram 27*). The dimension of the tenon should be the same as the mortise.

The mortise is cut first. If it is located near the end of the timber it is advisable to apply a C-cramp to prevent splitting. Secure the leg to the bench and remove as much of the waste as possible with a brace and bit. The bit should be slightly smaller than the width of the mortise (*diagram 28*). When doing this, view the bit from the end of the component as this will help keep the cut parallel to the face side (*diagram 29*). The remaining waste is then taken out with the mortise chisel, starting at the centre and gradually working outwards, with the final cuts being made on the marked lines. Take care when making these last cuts not to lever out the waste as this will round over the corners of the mortise and may in some instances be visible in the final construction. Masking tape wrapped around the drill bit and mortise chisel is used to denote the depth of cut (*diagram 30*).

masking tape

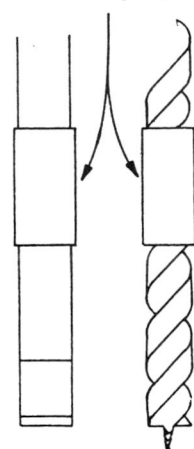

Diagram 30 *Masking tape wrapped around the mortise chisel and drill bit denotes the depth of cut.*

To cut the tenon, secure the rail in the vice at an angle of about 45° and away from the saw (*diagram 31*). With the blade working on the waste side of the line, start the cut on the corner and saw horizontally down to the shoulder,

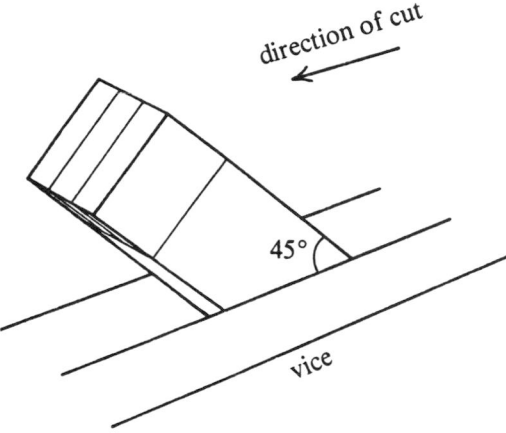

direction of cut

45°

vice

Diagram 31 *The rail is held in the vice at an angle of 45°, and away from the saw.*

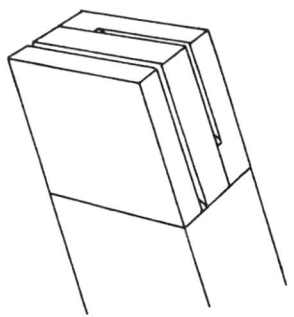

checking continually to ensure that the blade keeps to its path (*diagram 32*). Move the rail into the vertical position, and complete the cut using the existing saw kerf as a guide. Vertical cuts have also to be made at the shoulder line (*diagram 33*). Care should be taken when approaching the shoulder as any cut beyond it will result in a permanent flaw. The waste is then removed by making cuts on all four sides, leaving about 1mm (¹⁄₁₆in.) of waste. This is then removed by placing a paring chisel in the knifeline of the shoulder and chopping down to the tenon, making sure to keep the blade square to the face side. This method gives a clean, crisp shoulder superior to alternative types.

With all cutting operations complete, the joint should go together with slight pressure, its entry being assisted by chamfering the end of the tenon (*diagram 34*). An efficient joint will result if accuracy is maintained; a loose joint will provide little strength, while a tight fit may split the mortise.

Diagram 32 *Diagonal sawcuts are made on the waste side of the line from the outside corner to the opposite inside shoulder.*

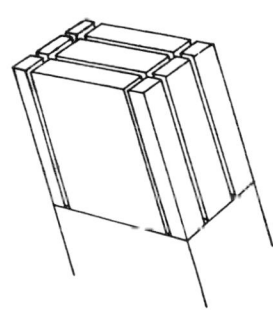

Diagram 33 *All sawcuts are made down to the shoulder line.*

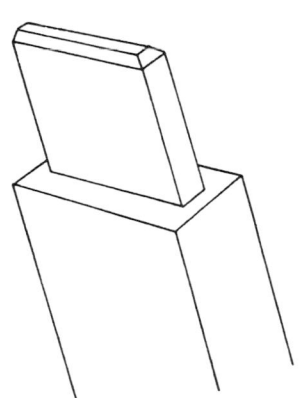

Diagram 34 *The tenon's entry is assisted by chamfering its end.*

Diagram 35 *Faults in constructing the mortise and tenon joint: 1. Undercut shoulders caused by cutting the tenon's shoulder incorrectly. 2. Overtight tenon causes the mortise to split. 3. Sawcuts taken beyond the shoulder lines of the tenon. 4. Shoulders of the tenon are uneven.*

A number of faults may cause the joint to be inefficient (*diagram 35*).

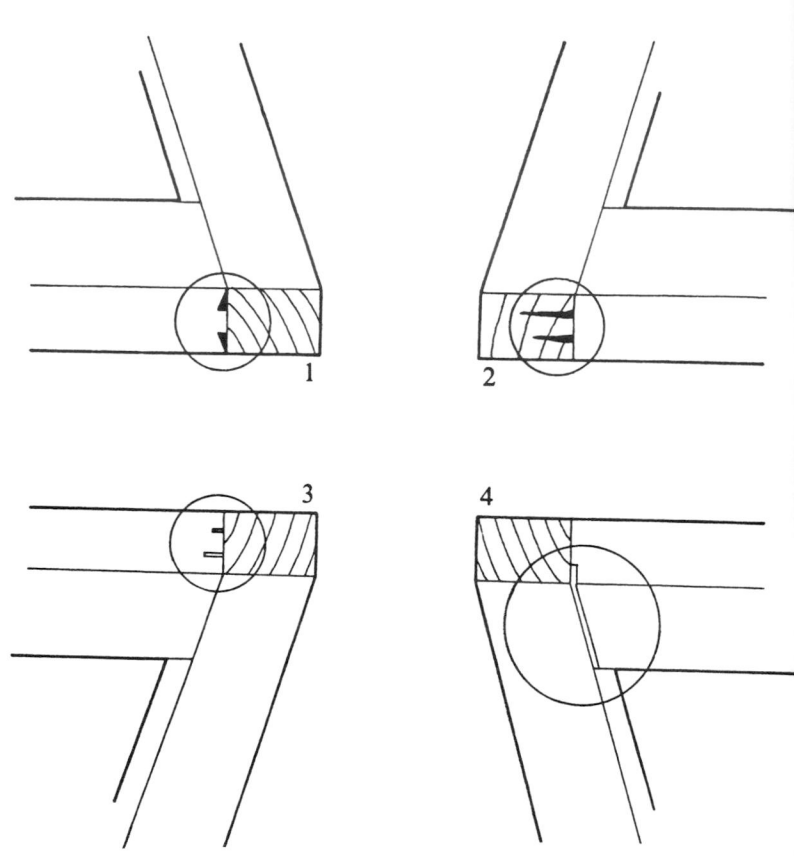

The method of draw-boring can be applied to the joint and is used to pull its shoulders together as well as to lock it. A dowel passes through the joint, the holes being slightly offset so that a compressive force is created. When the joint has been fitted, bore a hole through the mortice using waste material to prevent timber break out. Cramp the joint together and press the drill bit into the hole so that a centre mark is made on the tenon. Remove the tenon, and bore a hole through it slightly nearer the shoulder than the mark (*diagram 36*). A dowel with a heavily tapered end will allow easy access to the staggered holes and considerably tighten the joint when driven in (*diagram 37*).

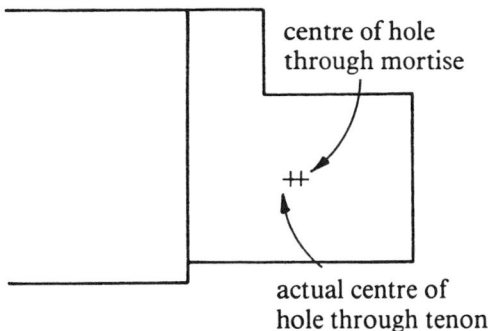

centre of hole
through mortise

actual centre of
hole through tenon

Diagram 36 *The hole in the tenon is drilled slightly nearer the shoulder than that through the mortise.*

Through mortise with securing wedges

A much improved type of mortise and tenon joint uses a through mortise with securing wedges to give additional mechanical strength (*diagram 38* and *figure 1*). The general procedure for marking out is repeated with the exception of the mortise, the lines being taken to both edges.

Cutting of the mortise is done from both sides rather than attempting to cut all the way through from one side, as this may result in timber breakout. The mortise has to be tapered from the outside to allow the tenon to spread when the

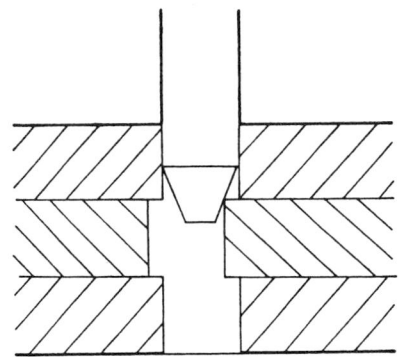

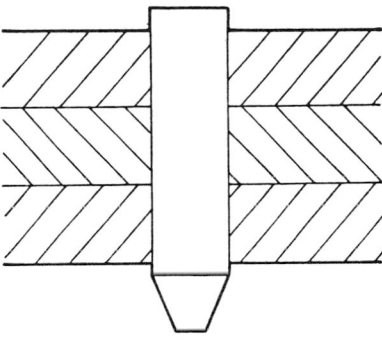

Diagram 37 *A heavily tapered dowel driven through the staggered holes will pull the joint together.*

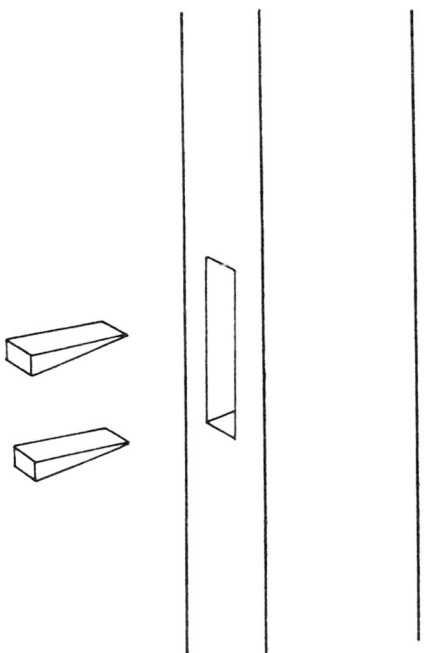

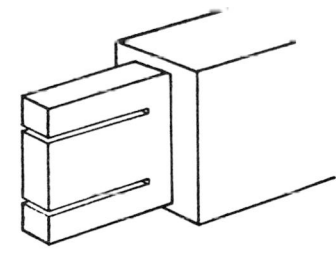

Diagram 38 *The through mortise and tenon with securing wedges.*

21

Figure 1 *Through mortise and tenon with securing wedges.*

wedges are driven in. This should start about 6mm (¼in.) from the inside edge and lengthen the mortise by 6mm (¼in.), although measurements will vary depending on the size of joint (*diagram 39*).

Diagram 39 *Section through the rail showing how the mortise is shaped to accept the wedges.*

Diagram 40 *Sawcuts made in the tenon to accept both wedges.*

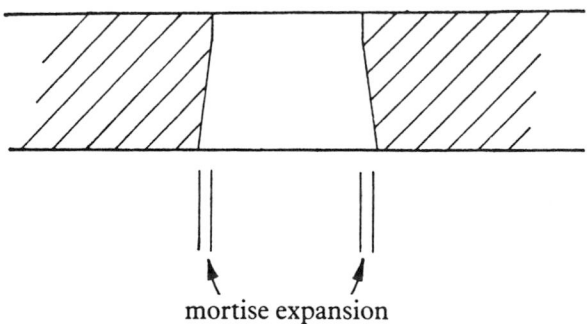

mortise expansion

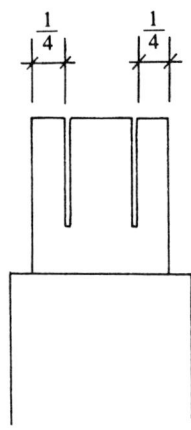

The tenon is made slightly longer than the mortise depth to allow for trimming after construction. The sawcuts that receive the wedges should be set in from the outer edge by one-quarter of the tenon width and terminate 6mm (¼in.) from the shoulder (*diagram 40*). The wedges can be made in a contrasting timber, but care should be taken to ensure that they are the same size and driven in an equal amount (*diagram 41*).

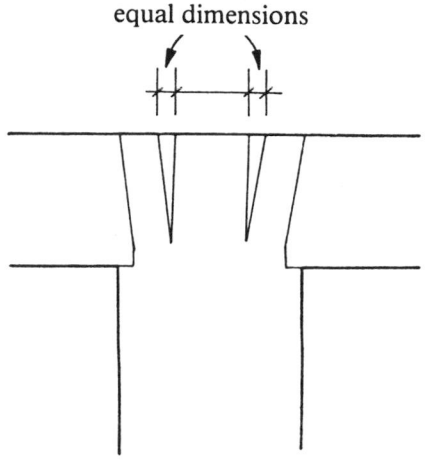

equal dimensions

Diagram 41 *Both wedges should have the same thickness on the outside after construction.*

Fox-wedged mortise and tenon

A similar joint that uses a stopped rather than a through mortice is called the fox-wedged mortise and tenon (*diagram 42*) and is used when the strength of wedging is required but a through mortise is undesirable. Great care must be taken in its construction if it is to perform at its best.

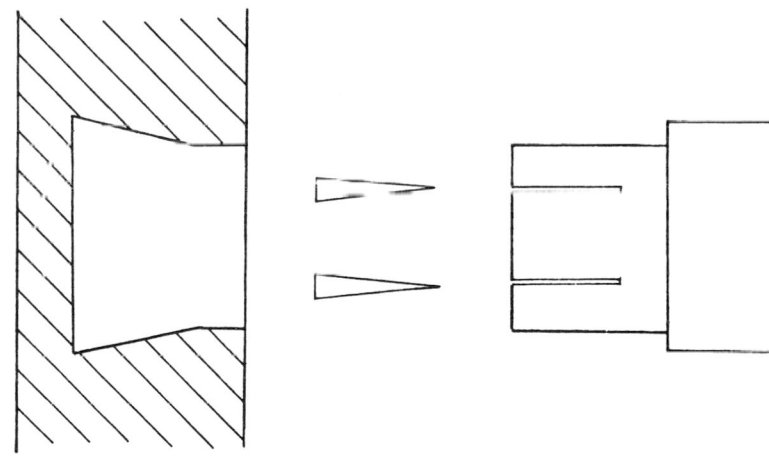

Diagram 42 *Fox-wedged mortise and tenon.*

Diagram 43 *The wedges should spread the tenon to fill the mortise as the shoulder meets the rail edge.*

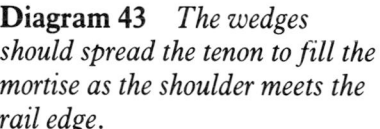

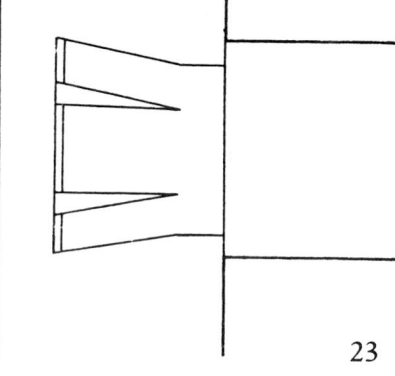

The process of cutting a standard mortise and tenon (*diagram 25, p. 17*) is carried out initially. The mortise is adjusted by undercutting its ends, starting about 6mm (¼in.) in from the edge, spreading the length by a further 6mm (¼in.) (*diagram 43*). When the wedges are inserted into the sawcuts, the tenon has to spread out to fill the mortise as the shoulder butts up to the edge. Faults obviously occur if either the wedges are so thin that the mortise is not filled or they are too thick and the mortise is filled before the shoulder closes up (*diagram 44*).

Diagram 44 *If the wedges are too thick, the mortise will be filled before the joint is together. Alternatively, if the wedges are too thin, the tenon will not fill the mortise.*

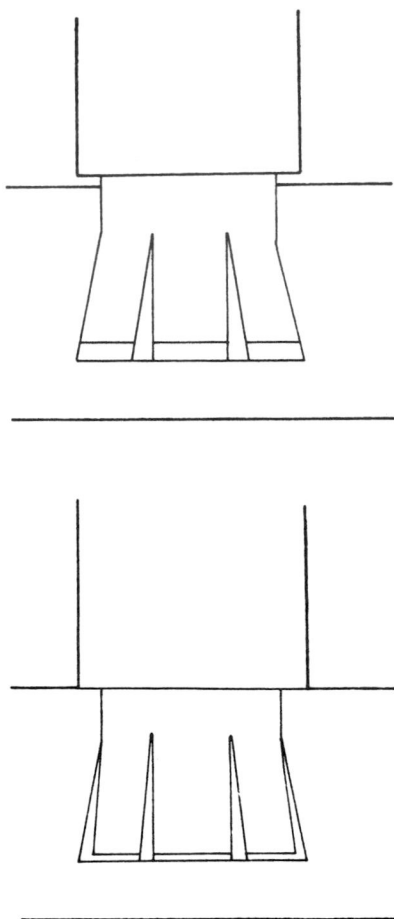

Diagram 45 *Short grain results if a rail is curved.*

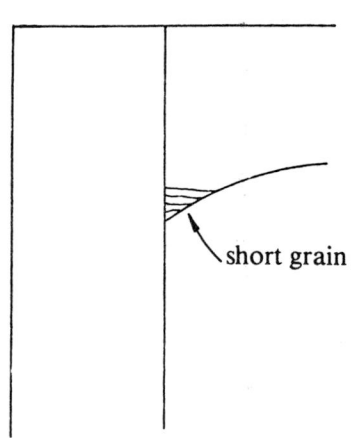

short grain

Gunstock mortise and tenon

Adaptations of the tenon shoulder are needed, for example when the rail is curved (*diagram 45*). If the square shoulder is used, short grain will occur at the end of the curve making it particularly weak. To compensate for this, the mitred shoulder is used with the joint being called a gunstock mortise and tenon (*diagram 46*). Two variations of the shoulder can be used.

The standard haunched mortise and tenon is made, allowing an additional 6mm (¼in.) on the tenon's shoulder to accept the mitre. This is marked in with a sliding bevel and knife (*diagram 47*). The joint is pushed together to mark the

24

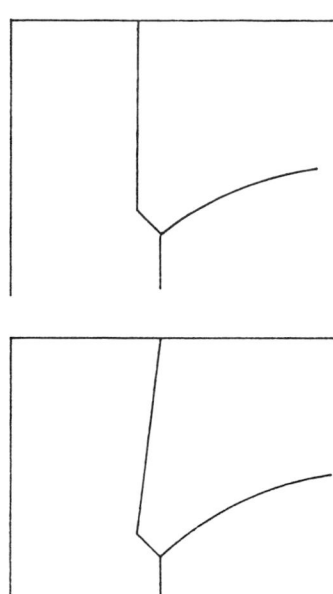

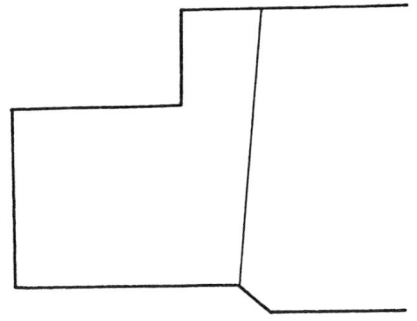

Diagram 47 *The shoulder of the tenoned component is marked in with a knife and sliding bevel.*

Diagram 46 *Two versions of the gunstock mortise and tenon.*

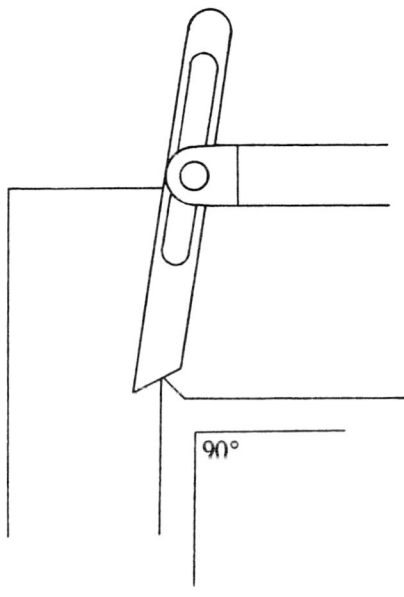

90°

angle on the mortised component and so its internal corner should be a right angle (*diagram 48*). The shoulder can then be cut and the joint fitted.

Diagram 48 *Ensure that the internal angle of the leg and rail is at 90° when marking the shoulder of the mortise.*

GROOVES AND REBATES

It often occurs when constructing a frame that a panel of some sort has to be included which requires the cutting of a groove or rebate. This is made easier by adjusting the joint to allow a through, rather than a stopped, rebate or groove.

When using a groove, its dimensions should ideally be the same as the square haunch so that they can be cut together (*diagram 49*). It can be made smaller than the haunch but anything larger will mean removing timber that should be retained.

A rebate requires much more adjustment of the joint to allow easy cutting. If it is cut in a standard mortise and tenoned frame, the shoulder of one side of the mortise will be removed (*diagram 50*). This has to be filled by adjusting the

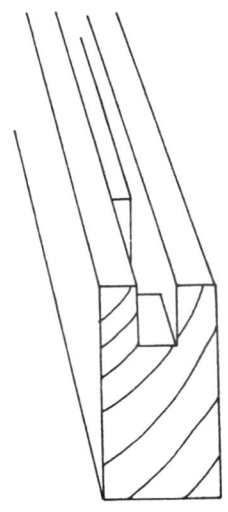

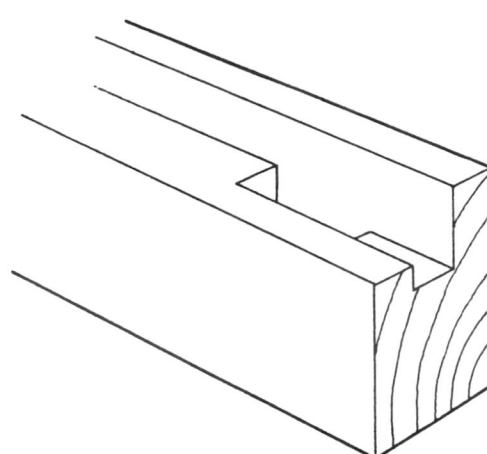

Diagram 50 *One side of the mortise is removed when a rebate is c*

Diagram 49 *Ideally, the groove should be the same width as the mortise.*

Diagram 51 *The long-and-short-shouldered mortise and tenon joint.*

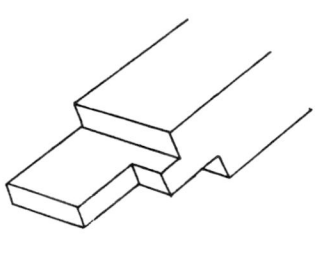

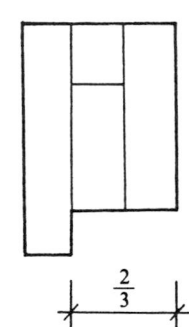

Diagram 52 *The rebate should be two-thirds the rail thickness and flush with the tenon's face.*

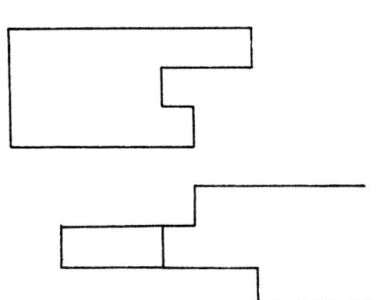

Diagram 53 *The back shoulder is extended by the rebate width.*

shoulder of the tenoned component, the resulting adaptation being called a long-and-short-shouldered mortise and tenon (*diagram 51*).

The rebate should be two-thirds the thickness of the rail and line up with the face of the tenon (*diagram 52*). Having made the mortise, use a rebate or plough plane to cut the through rebate, making sure that its fence is always pressed tightly against the timber as any deviation may result in a step forming in the corner. Any final trimming that may be necessary can be done with a shoulder plane.

Adjustment of the tenon is achieved by extending the back shoulder by the width of the rebate (*diagram 53*). The initial shoulder line is only marked in lightly as a temporary measure. The long shoulder is then found by cramping the faces of the two adjoining components together and marking it from the inside of the rebate (*diagram 54*). The width of the tenon is determined by the depth of the rebate, and should not be so deep that the strength of the joint is affected (*diagram 55*).

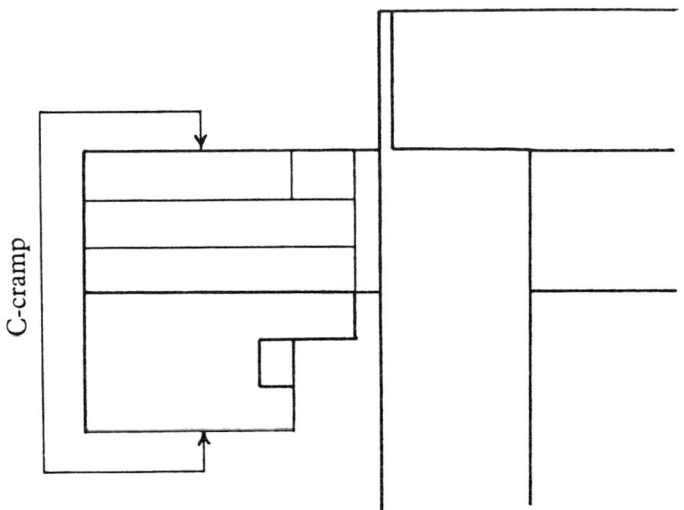

C-cramp

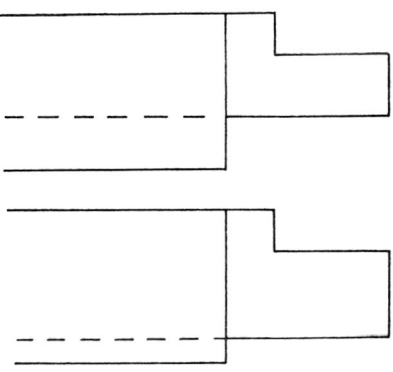

Diagram 54 *Cramp two adjoining rails together to mark in the length of the shoulder extension.*

Diagram 55 *Too wide a rebate will reduce the strength of the tenon. The lower diagram shows appropriate proportions.*

DRY JOINTING

In Eastern societies, the joint was a very important part of the total design in both furniture and architecture. The use of dry joinery (glue was not used) was the mainstay of their constructions, with locking components predominating. These required the design of intricate configurations that had a high strength factor. The craftsmen maintained total accuracy and a range of joints was achieved which were unsurpassed in their technical excellence.

It is clear from extant examples of Chinese furniture that the two types of construction most widely used were the panelled frame and the joint used to attach the leg to a table top. A typical frame (*diagram 56*) illustrates the basic elements of Chinese joinery and is a good example of a mitred, mortise and tenon frame with dovetailed transverse brace and tongue and grooved floating panels. This method of framing was used extensively for cabinet construction in doors, tops, sides and backs, varying in degrees of refinement according to the object's intended environment.

Diagram 56 *The typical type of frame used in Chinese furniture.*

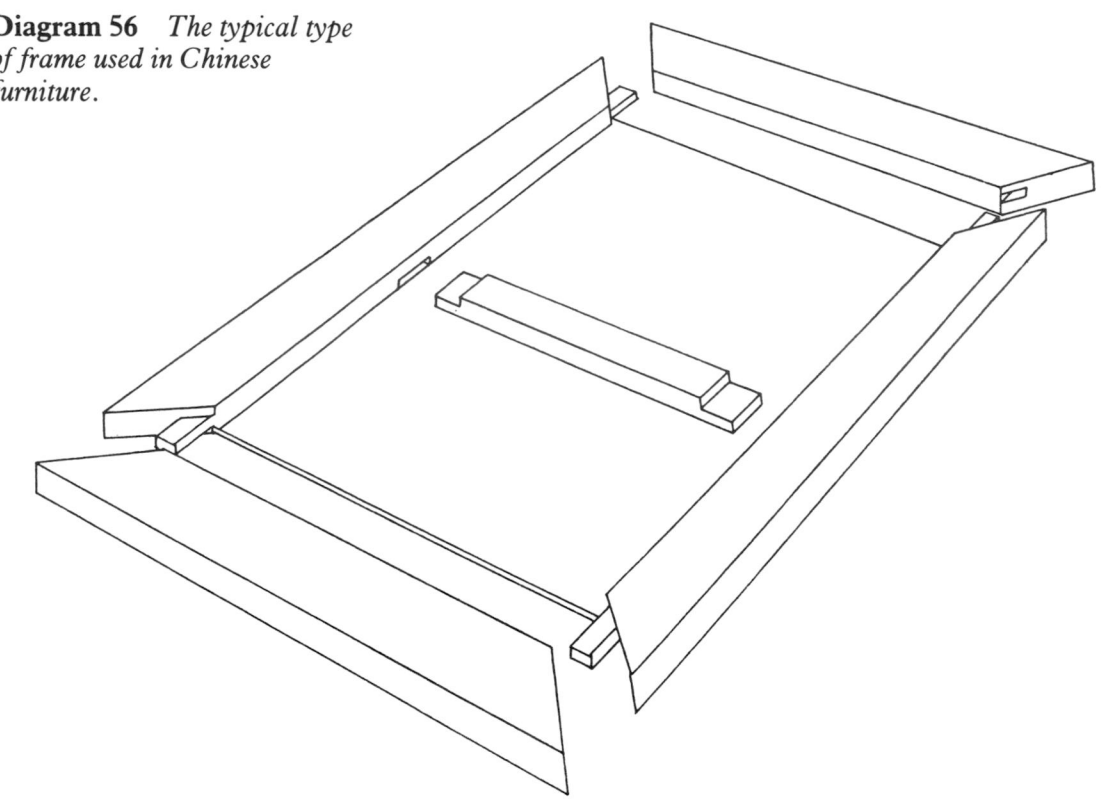

Chinese mortise and tenon

The corner joint used in this type of frame, though a simple form of mortise and tenon, is important because of its frequent use in Chinese furniture. It is also a good platform on which to base one's knowledge of how the Eastern style of joinery was constructed (*diagram 57, figure 2*).

Having prepared all the components, the mitres are marked on each end, working from the face side and face edge (*diagram 58*). The through mortise can then be marked in, the inside shoulder line being the same as the mitres and its width being one-third the thickness of the rail. Set the mortise gauge so that its points are symmetrical, and scribe lines on both edges. Its length is one-third the width of the rail (*diagram 59*).

The tenon is marked out in virtually the same way, the gauge being used at the same setting to scribe its thickness on the inside edge and end of the rail. Its width is measured from

28

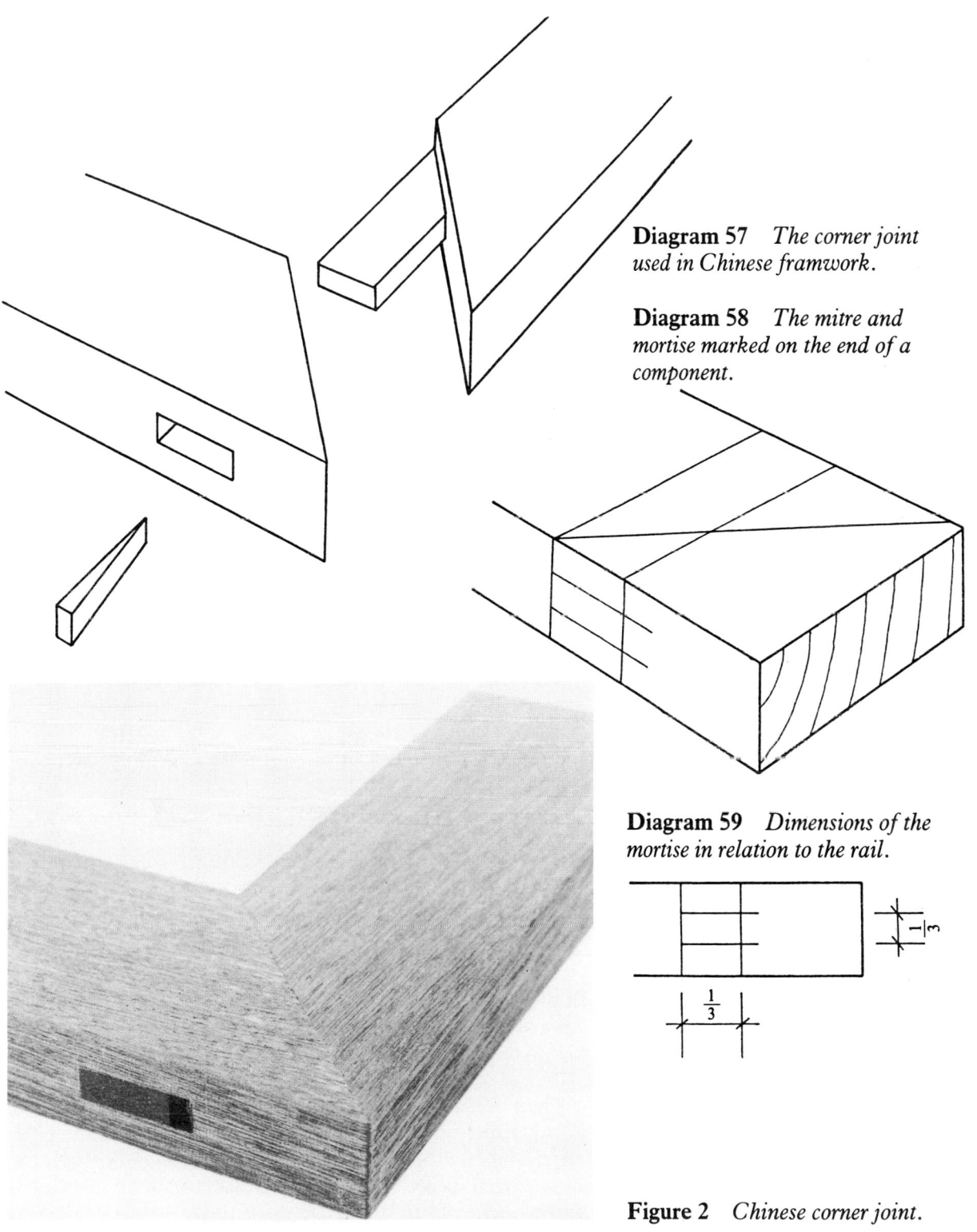

Diagram 57 *The corner joint used in Chinese framwork.*

Diagram 58 *The mitre and mortise marked on the end of a component.*

Diagram 59 *Dimensions of the mortise in relation to the rail.*

Figure 2 *Chinese corner joint.*

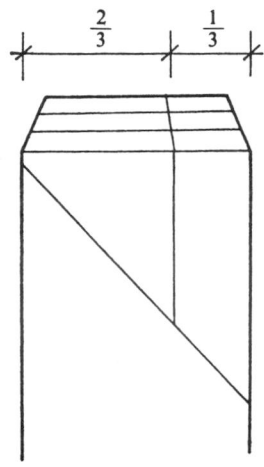

the mortise and scribed with a marking gauge from the edge (*diagram 60*).

To avoid removing the outline of the joint, cut the mortise before the mitre. This should be done from both sides, as described when cutting the through mortise and tenon with securing wedges (*diagram 38, p. 21*). The mortise should only be enlarged on the outside end to allow access for the wedge (*diagram 61*). The final operation on this part of the joint is to

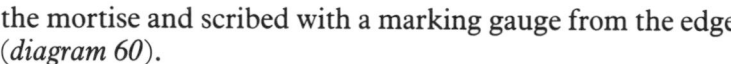

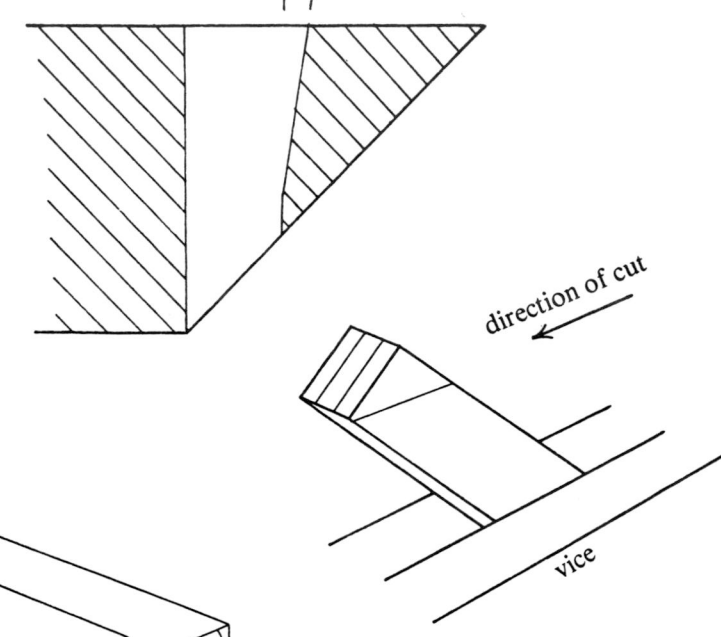

Diagram 60   *The tenon width is one-third that of the rail and scribed from the inside edge.*

Diagram 61   *The mortise should only be enlarged on the outside end to accept the wedge.*

Diagram 62   *Mitre shooting board.*

Diagram 63   *The component is placed in the vice with the mitre line in a horizontal position.*

cut the mitre. Most of the waste can be sawn away, leaving a slight amount for trimming. The ideal method of planing back to the shoulder is to use a mitre shooting board (*diagram 62*).

When forming the tenon, all sawcuts should be made before removing any waste as this process may eliminate the gauge lines. As there are only two surfaces to work from, the rail is placed in the vice with the mitre line in an horizontal position (*diagram 63*) and cuts are made to the shoulder.

30

Then move the rail into the vertical position and make the cut that gives the tenon width. Waste is then removed by cutting around the mitre. This can be trimmed back with a paring chisel, keeping it square to the face side.

Both mitres should be checked across the width for flatness as any projection in the middle will prevent the joint fitting on the outside. This will occur if the chisel is not held square when removing the waste (*diagram 64*).

If all the cutting has been carried out accurately then the joint should go together with light pressure. If there are any particularly tight areas, further removal of waste is needed. When the joint fits comfortably, pull the mitre together and drive in the wedge. Any protrusion of the tenon can then be planed flush to the outer edge.

Three-way mitre

The joint described above was the foundation of many Chinese furniture designs, and there were, inevitably, variations on the basic theme. By introducing another rail, a three-way mitre can be made, giving a clean and simple outer appearance, that is joined by a system of mortise and tenons on the inside (*diagram 65*). The three rails have to be square so that all outer angles are 45°.

The construction of the horizontal frame is similar to the previous example, with a difference in size and placement of the tenon being the only major change. Its thickness is now one-quarter of the rail thickness and is placed above the centre line (*diagram 66*). This change is essential in order to avoid the mitre that will be cut to accept the vertical component.

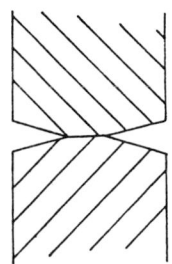

Diagram 64 *Enlarged sectional view of the mitre showing a protrusion at the centre, preventing the joint meeting on the outside.*

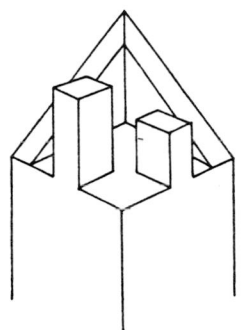

Diagram 65 *Vertical component showing the mortise configuration of a three-way mitre.*

Diagram 66 *The dimensions of the tenon which is placed above the centre line.*

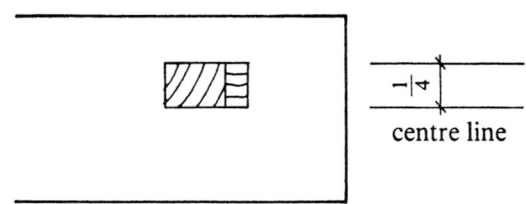

centre line

When marking out the joint that connects the vertical member to the horizontal frame, care must be taken to ensure that the mortise does not run out into the mitre. To achieve this, the end grain should be scribed into five equal divisions with the mortise gauge (*diagram 67*).

Two other variations show a simple oval leg tenoned into the framed top (*diagram 68*), and an elaborate construction

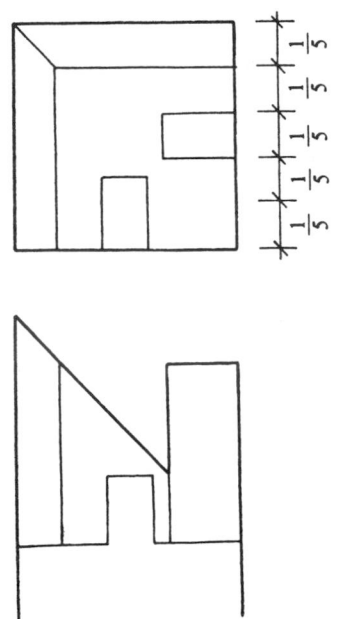

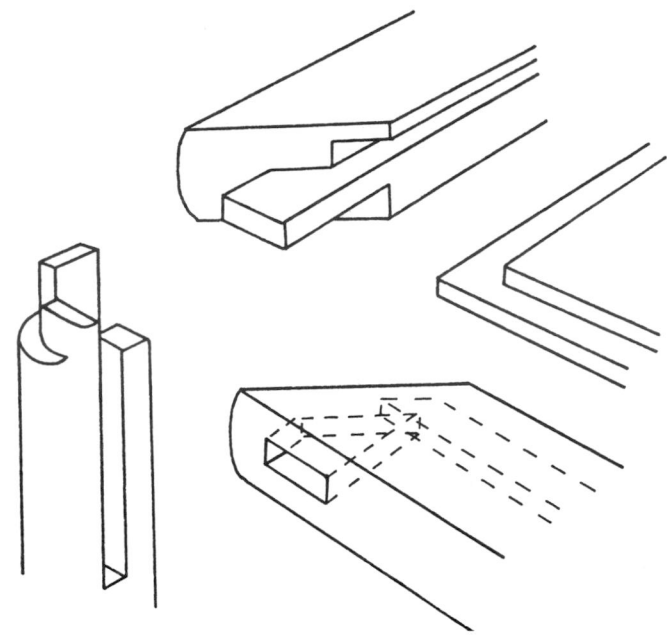

Diagram 67 *The end grain of the vertical component is divided into five equal parts when marking in the joint.*

Diagram 68 *Simple oval leg tenoned into a framed top.*

where the addition of a rail and complex shaping creates the distinctive style established by the Chinese craftsman (*diagram 69*).

Chinese and Japanese craftsmen developed a vast repertoire of joinery for any situation that might arise, the common feature being some form of mechanical locking device. Inevitably the dovetail-shaped tenon played a major role in many of these joints.

Diagram 69 *The elaborate form of leg joint used in a table of distinctive Chinese style.*

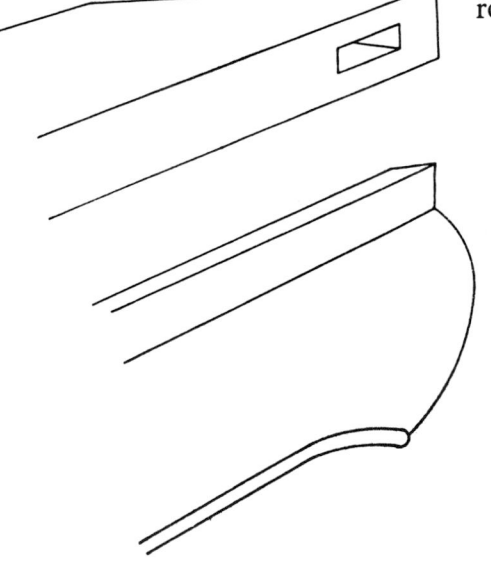

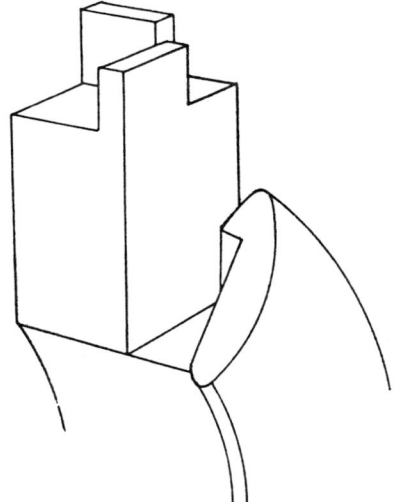

Slide-lock mortise and tenon

Having built the panelled frame, the craftsman had to find some method of joining the pieces together to create a carcase. The wedge-shaped, slide-lock mortise and tenon (*diagram 70*) was devised for such an occasion, usually for large pieces of furniture meant to be readily disassembled for easy transportation.

The locking component (*diagram 71*) is cut independently of both adjoining panels, and is then permanently tenoned into one, while slide locking into the other. This should be made first and all subsequent dimensions taken from it. Its dimensions depend on the size of panels being joined, but are generally found as follows: length equals three-quarters the width of rail in panel one, plus three-quarters the thickness of rail in panel two; width is dependent on panel size, but is half the length of the mortise; and thickness equals one-third the thickness of panel one (*diagram 72*). When the timber is cut to these dimensions, the only shaping to be done is to remove a small wedge from each side to create the locking

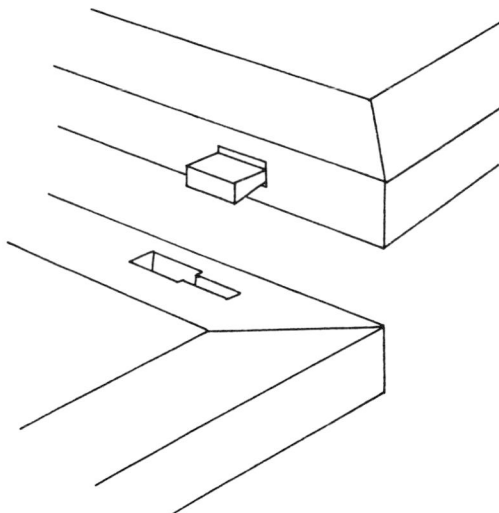

Diagram 70   *The wedge-shaped, slide-lock mortise and tenon.*

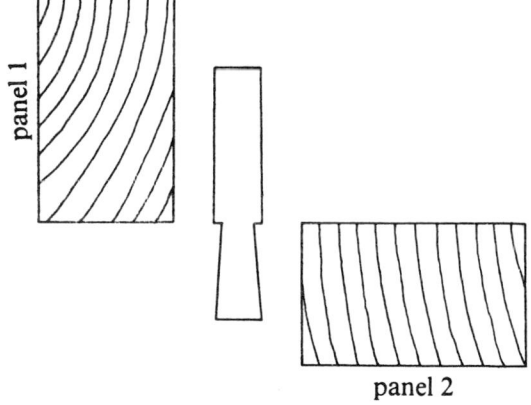

panel 1

panel 2

Diagram 72   *Proportions of the locking component in relation to adjacent rails.*

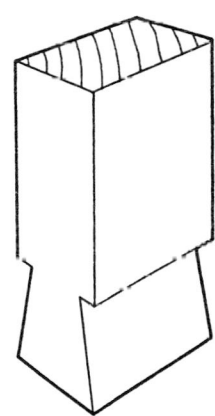

Diagram 71   *The locking component.*

mechanism. Its length should be equal to three-quarters the thickness of panel two, measured from the end (*diagram 73*). The dimensions of each mortise can be taken from the locking component and scribed on to the panel rails; note that the vertical panel is stepped in by 3mm (⅛in.) from the edge of the horizontal panel.

The locking component should be first glued into the mortise of the vertical panel. The mortise on the horizontal panel is cut so that the wedge-shaped half terminates at the

Diagram 73   *Shaded areas denote waste timber that has to be removed.*

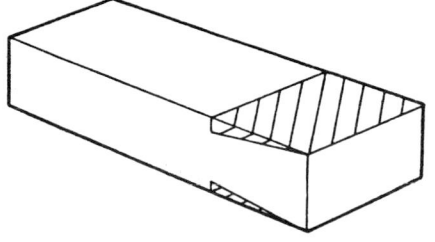

33

same distance from the edge of the panel as does the tenon (*diagram 74*). This ensures that the carcase will be flush at the

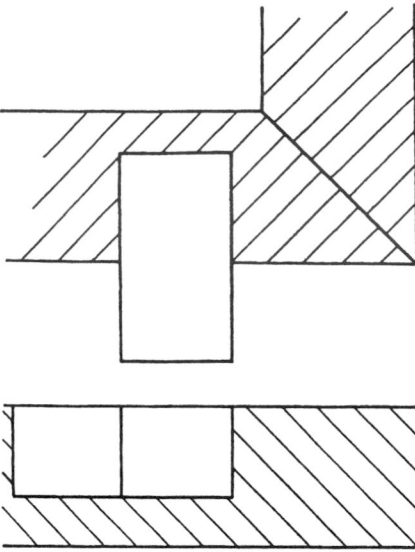

Diagram 74 *Section through each rail showing the locking component in position and its adjacent mortise.*

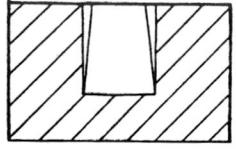

Diagram 75 *Section of the mortised rail.*

front when put together. The mortise is cut twice as long as the tenon width, one half being square and the other half being narrower at the surface but fully square on the inside (*diagram 75*). This allows the tenons to drop into one half and slide into the V-shaped section, locking the tenon in position.

Japanese *Sage kama*

The development of Japanese architectural style followed a similar pattern in its use of dry-jointing methods. To resist lateral forces, rails were used rather than the diagonal bracing associated with Western architecture. Rails and tie-beams served the normal function of horizontal bracing, giving rigidity to a framework and strengthening posts under compressive loads. These rails were subject to stress and so required joints that not only remained strong under tension but could be made without the excessive removal of timber which would reduce efficiency. The *Sage kama* (wedged through half dovetail; *diagram 76* and *figure 3*) fills these requirements. The half dovetail of the rail effectively hangs on the mortise, providing a very tight joint as the wedge is driven in which cannot slip or be pulled out.

Rails used in Japanese constructions were generally 25 x 150mm (1 x 6in.) or 50 x 250mm (2 x 10in.), which meant that a small amount of cutting to create a joint would quickly

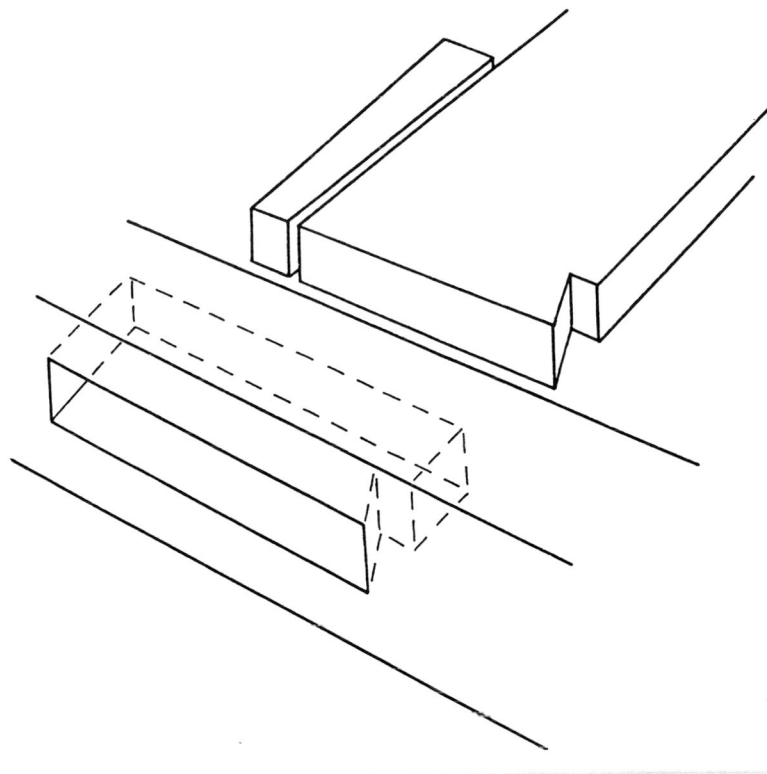

Diagram 76   Saga-kama
(*wedged through half dovetail
joint*).

Figure 3   Sage-kama (*wedged
through half dovetail*)

35

cause weakness. *Sage kama* was probably designed to be the least destructive method of joining rail to post and, therefore, the most effective way of maintaining stability. The compression of the joint created by the introduction of the wedge makes it better adapted to resist tension stress than other forms of connection. The same principles apply on much lighter structures, which makes the *Sage kama* the ideal joint to use on stretchers in knock down chairs and tables.

Generally the *Sage kama* uses a post that is three times the thickness of the rail. The rail should be cut to the same thickness as a suitable mortise chisel because the mortise will be barefaced. This is initially cut to the same dimension as the rail and then shaped at each end to allow access for the wedge and dovetail (*diagram 77*). The upper end is cut at an

Diagram 77 *Section of the mortised rail showing necessary adjustments to accept the rail and wedge.*

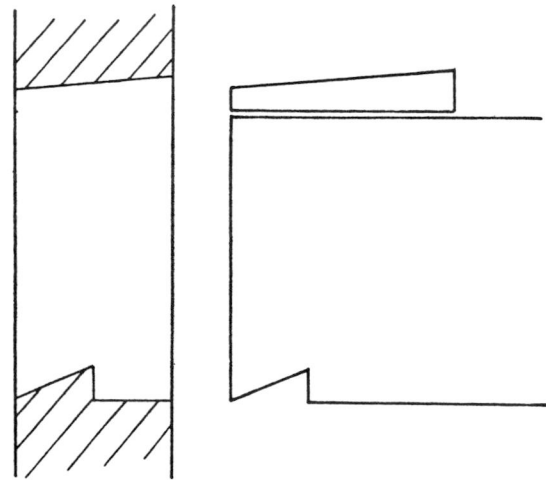

angle of 10°, reducing the mortise length towards the outside. The lower end has the same shoulderline on the outside surfaces, but is cut to accept the dovetail. The inner half is cut square while the outer half is tapered at the same angle as the dovetail (about 1:6). The rail merely requires the removal of a wedge-shaped section to match the shaping of the mortise. The joint can then be pushed together and a wedge cut and fitted to secure it.

Ari-otoshi (housed dovetail joint)
A similar joint, *Ari-otoshi* (housed dovetail joint; *diagram 78*), was used on a much wider rail with the full dovetail fitted to a blind mortise. The first step in constructing the joint should

36

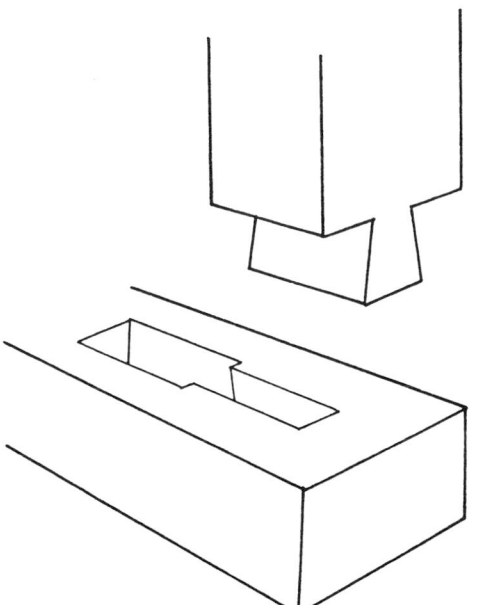

Diagram 78 Ari-otoshi
(*housed dovetail joint*).

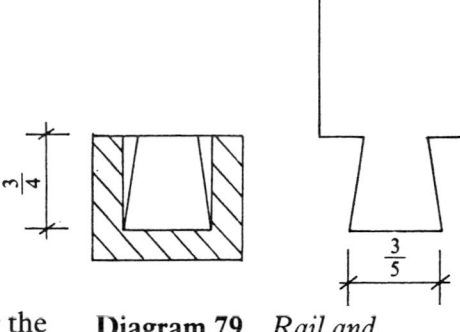

Diagram 79 *Rail and
sectioned post showing the relative
proportions of the joint.*

be to cut the dovetailed rail so that all measurements for the mortise can be taken from it. A sliding bevel is set at an angle of 1:6 and used to mark the dovetail from the square-ended rail. The shoulder is set in from the end by three-quarters of the post's thickness. The tail width is three-fifths of the rail (*diagram 79*).

The upper half of the mortise must be the same dimension as the end of the tail and should be square, while the lower half is cut to the shape of the tail (*diagram 80*). Both parts of the mortise are initially cut square with the lower half then being cut back at an angle of 1:6. By making this part of the mortise slightly shorter than the thickness of the rail, compressive pressure is exerted when the securing wedge is driven in.

Kamasen-uchi (gooseneck mortise and tenon)

The next logical step in the development of a locking joint is to produce a construction that gives the effect of a rail protruding from both sides of the post. This was achieved by using the *kamasen-uchi* (gooseneck mortise and tenon; *diagram 81*) which uses a spliced rail set in a through mortise.

Cramp the two rails together and mark in the shoulderline which should be less than the thickness of the post by 6mm (¼in.). Set the mortise gauge to one-quarter of the rail width and scribe the neck of the joint centrally from shoulder to end. At the point where these lines meet the end, using a sliding bevel set at 1:5, scribe in the tapered end; this should

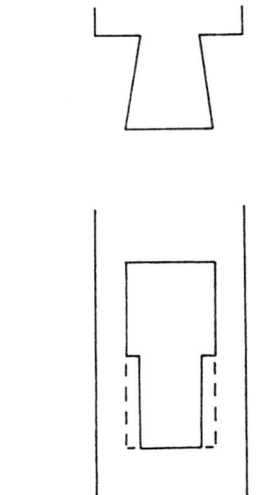

Diagram 80 *One-half of the
mortise is shaped to the same
angle as the dovetailed rail.*

37

Diagram 81 Kamasen-uchi
(gooseneck mortise and tenon joint).

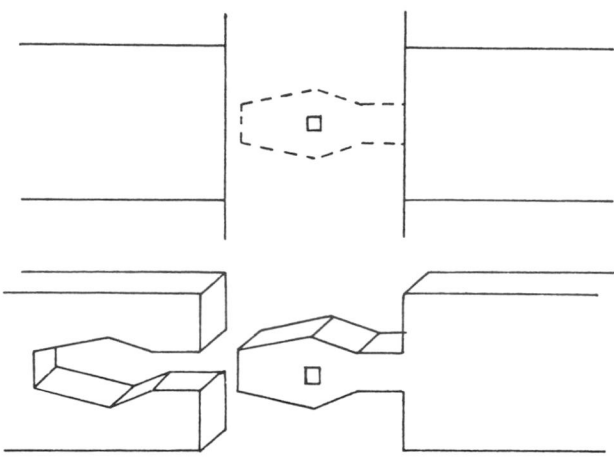

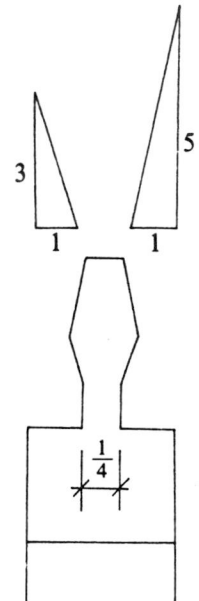

Diagram 82 *Outline of the gooseneck with relative angles.*

be one-half the rail width at its widest point. The outline is completed by taking this point back to the neck at an angle of 1:3 (*diagram 82*). This part of the joint can then be cut, making sure that the edges always remain square.

Using the gooseneck as a template, place it on top of the adjoining rail, with its end on the shoulderline, and scribe in the joint (*diagram 83*). To remove the waste, use a drill of suitable size to cut the head and then saw down the neck to connect the end with it. The internal faces can then be trimmed back and the two rails fitted.

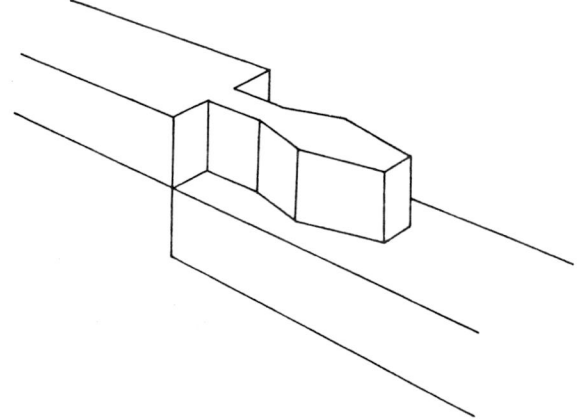

Diagram 83 *The gooseneck is used as a template to scribe the adjoining rail.*

Prior to cutting the through mortise, a round or square hole should be made to accept the securing peg; this operation is made easier if carried out at this stage. The mortise is then cut to accept the rail and, as it is barefaced, care should be taken to ensure that all corners remain square.

The joint is constructed by pushing the female member through the mortise so that its shoulder extends beyond the post, inserting the male component and pulling back the joint into the mortise. The hole is then extended through the rail and the peg driven in to lock the joint in position.

GLUED JOINTS

The common variations on the mortise and tenon have been discussed with the first hints of decoration seen in the use of contrasting wedges and dowels to help strengthen them. But what of the more visually interesting construction that can be used to replace these standard, usually secret joints? By introducing a combination of contrasting splines, dowels or pegs, a major decorative feature can be used that still has all the necessary strength expected from a joint. One of the most advanced ranges of joinery using this principle was designed by Charles and Henry Greene, who practised as architects in Pasadena, California, in the early part of this century. They made a conscious effort to create a visually expressive style that used the basic principles of construction, and this became one of the key characteristics of their architecture and furniture. The joinery varied considerably from the simple to the complex and the more complex it became, the further the principle developed.

Butt mitre with contrasting spline and dowels

One of the simplest joints uses a butt mitre in combination with a contrasting spline and dowels (*diagram 84* and *figure 4*). It is similar to a mitred bridle, the difference being that the spline is a separate, contrasting insert.

Mitres should be marked on the end of each rail, using the knife and sliding bevel, which are then cut and finished with the aid of a mitre shooting board (*diagram 62 on p. 30*). The spline should be approximately one-third the thickness of the rail but set to the nearest mortise chisel. If the exact size is not available, make the spline slightly thicker in order to improve the visual appearance of the joint.

The mortise is scribed centrally on the edge of the rail, extending beyond the inside shoulder by one-fifth the rail

Diagram 84 *The butt mitre in combination with contrasting spline and dowels.*

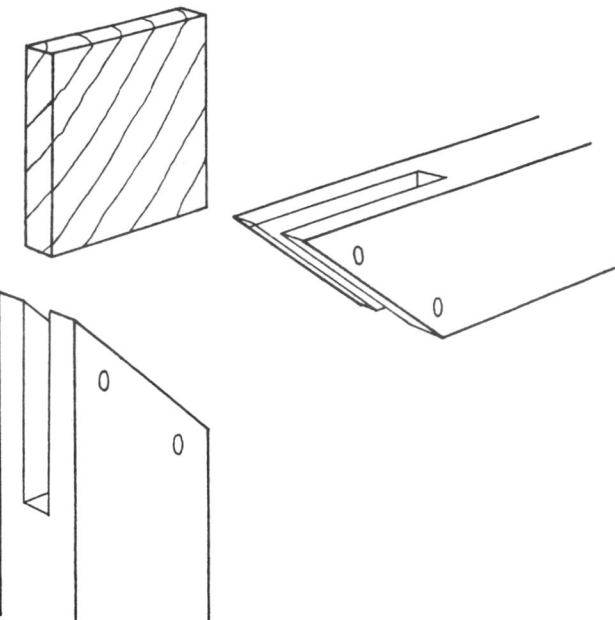

Figure 4 *Mitre in combination with contrasting spline and dowels.*

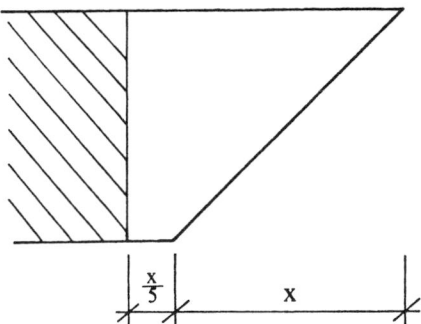

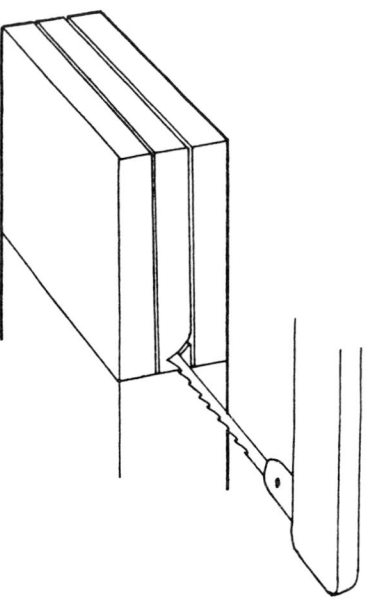

Diagram 85 *The inside shoulder of the mortise is extended beyond the inside shoulder of the mitre by one-fifth of the rail width.*

width (*diagram 85*). This extension increases the size of slip giving more material in which to locate the dowels.

The cutting of the joint is similar to that of a tenon but, as the central portion is to be removed, sawing is done on the inside of the gauge lines. The waste can be removed either with a coping saw or by drilling with a brace and bit, working from both sides (*diagram 86*). The shoulder is then trimmed with the mortise chisel. When both ends have been cut, a contrasting spline should be planed to the same thickness as the mortise with its grain running perpendicular to the mitre (*diagram 87*).

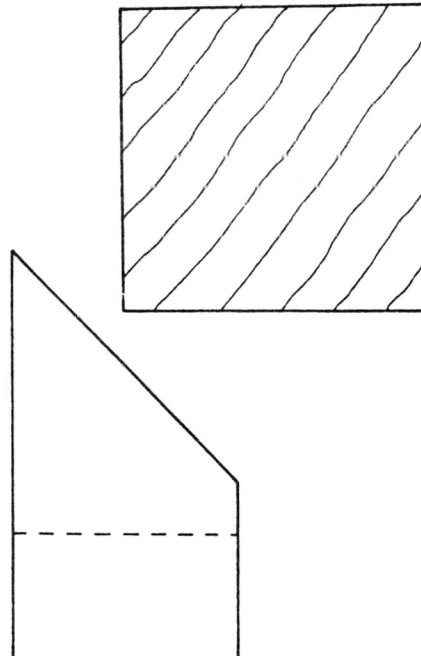

Diagram 86 *Removing the waste with a coping saw.*

Diagram 87 *The grain of the contrasting slip is perpendicular to the mitre line.*

Two holes are bored through the mortise, positioned within 1.2cm (½in.) of the edge, though the exact position

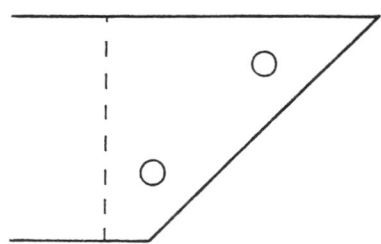

Diagram 88 *Position of holes to be bored through the mortise.*

depends on the size of joint (*diagram 88*). To avoid splitting the timber when drilling, a temporary filling is placed in the mortise and a waste piece cramped to the back.

When fitting the spline, cramp it up to the shoulder in one mortise and drill the holes, using those already cut, as a guide. This part of the joint can then be secured temporarily with dowels.

The fitting of the adjacent rail requires particularly accurate work because the mitre must meet at the same time as the spline butts up to the inside shoulder of the mortise. Place it on top of the protruding spline, holding the mitre together, and mark on the inside shoulder (*diagram 89*). This point is then squared round the spline and used as a guide to plane down to. Continually check the fit of the joint when planing to the line until it is located accurately.

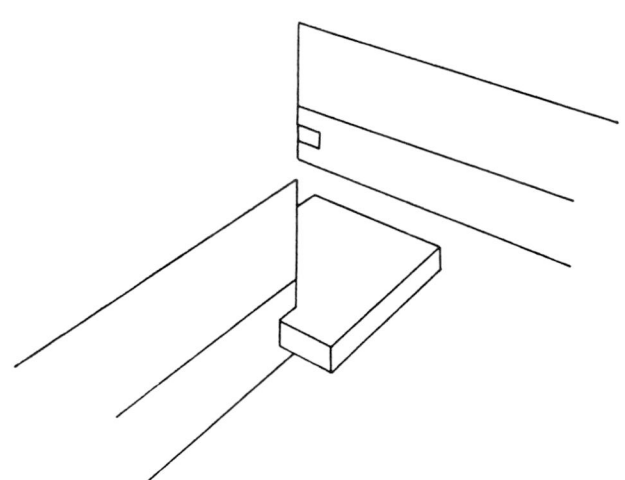

Diagram 89 *The adjacent rail is placed on top of the protruding spline to mark in the inside shoulder.*

When all necessary fitting is complete, it should be decided how to finish the spline and dowels; they can be either raised or planed flush to the rail. Visually, greater emphasis is placed on the joint if they are raised by about 3mm (⅛in.) with all sharp corners rounded prior to gluing. If a flush joint is required, any protrusions can be planed down after construction. The joint is visually improved by shaping the components as they approach the corner *figure 5*).

Square butt with dovetail-shaped spline
A joint that is both technically complex and more visually appealing uses the same basic principle of construction but

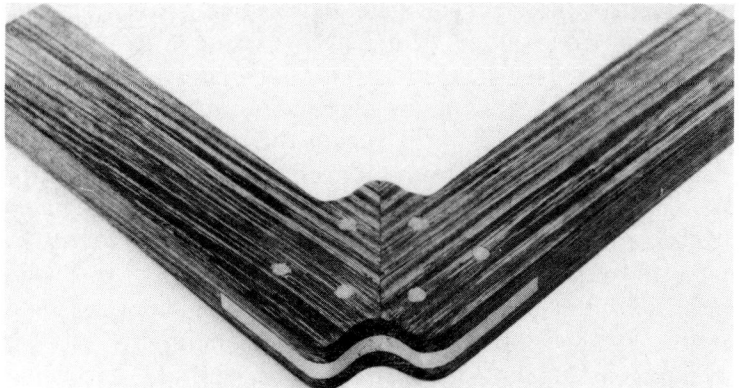

Figure 5 *Shaped components create further visual interest.*

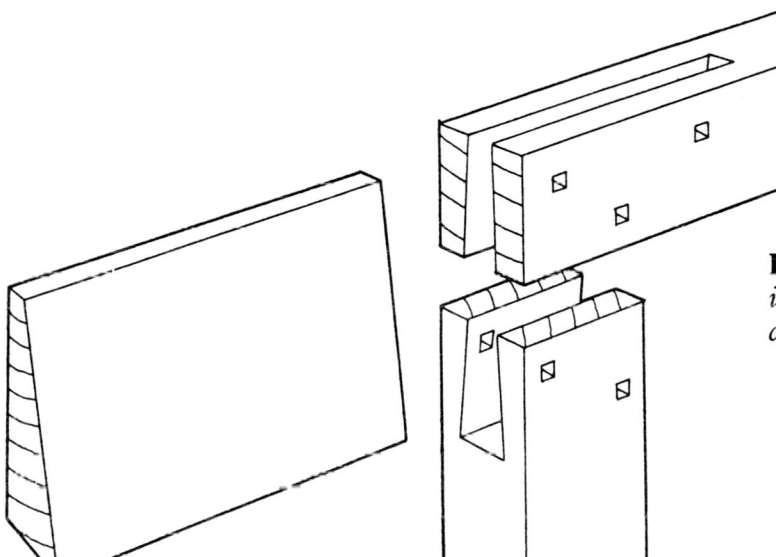

Diagram 90 *The square butt in conjunction with a contrasting dovetail spline and pegs.*

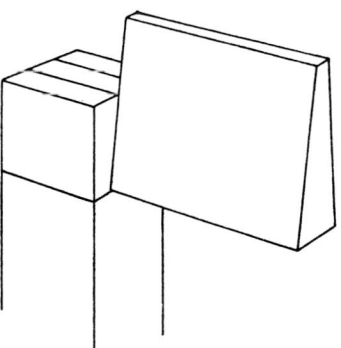

Diagram 91 *Use the dovetail spline as a template to mark the socket outline on the vertical component.*

has a dovetail-shaped spline with a square butt replacing the mitre (*diagram 90*).

The contrasting spline is made first; this should be twice the width of the horizontal component and twice as long as the vertical component. The dovetail angle depends on the size of joints, but is generally one-half the rail thickness at its widest, tapering down to one-quarter. To allow for cleaning up after construction, the spline should be made about 6mm (¼in.) longer and wider.

The socket in the vertical member is cut first. The inside shoulder is set in from the end and the spline used as a template to scribe its outline in a central position (*diagram 91*). Place the component in the vice with the scribed lines in

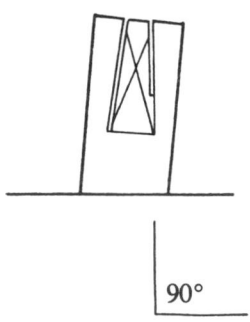

90°

Diagram 92 *Place the component in the vice so that the sawcut is made vertically.*

Diagram 93 *A rounded shoulder prevents the spline fitting on the outside edges.*

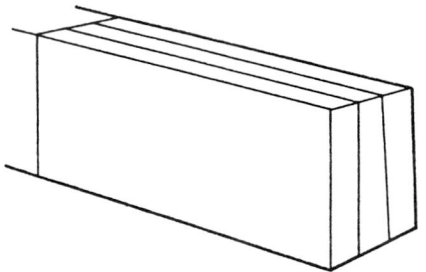

Diagram 94 *Having marked in the outline of the socket on the end grain, scribe parallel lines back to the shoulder line using a mortise gauge.*

a vertical position and cut down to the shoulder, working on the waste side, taking care not to deviate from the lines (*diagram 92*). The waste is then removed and any necessary trimming done with a paring chisel.

When the spline is in the socket the position of the pegs should be decided, with no more than three being used, to prevent the joint being weakened. The holes can then be drilled, placing waste timber in and behind the socket to prevent breakout. The square peg is visually superior in this joint and will require additional cutting. The spline is pulled tightly against the shoulder by using the draw-boring method to locate the pegs (*see diagram 37 on p. 21*). The spline is marked at the point where it emerges from the end of the socket and removed with this part complete.

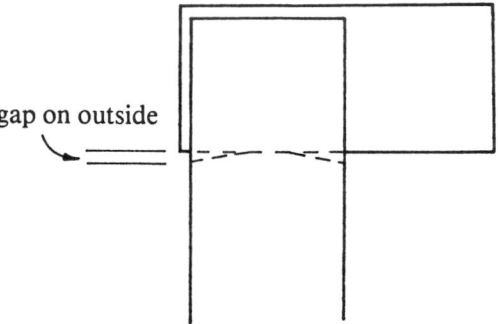

gap on outside

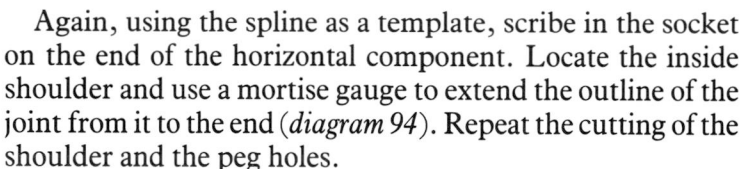

Again, using the spline as a template, scribe in the socket on the end of the horizontal component. Locate the inside shoulder and use a mortise gauge to extend the outline of the joint from it to the end (*diagram 94*). Repeat the cutting of the shoulder and the peg holes.

If the spline is to be left proud, cut it to within 3mm (⅛in.) of the inside and outside edges and round all sharp corners. The end of the horizontal component should be planed flush with the outer edge when the joint is together. The construction can be improved visually by shaping the components as they approach the joint.

The use of the contrasting spline is probably one of the most successful methods of creating a joint that is decorative and still has the necessary strength required to lock two components. The following examples show variations on this theme, using the spline to connect rails that meet with a butt or mitre. Methods of extending the decoration from joint to joint in a frame can also be introduced.

Splined mitre with contrasting inserts

The splined mitre (*diagram 95* and *figure 6*) can use any number of contrasting inserts, depending on the rail width, to create visual appeal, and is one of the simpler joints to construct. Before introducing the spline, the frame is constructed using simple, butt-mitred corners. In this example two splines are used with a thickness slightly less than one-fifth the rail width.

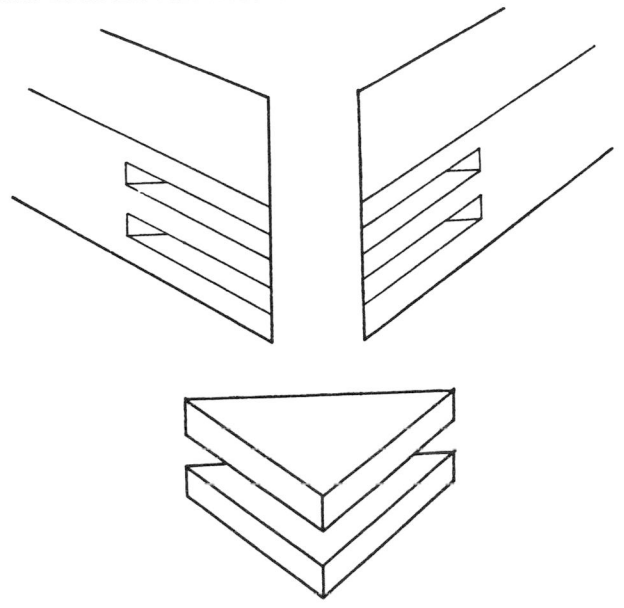

Diagram 95   *Splined mitre with two inserts.*

Figure 6   *Splined mitre.*

45

Diagram 96 *Socket depth is two-thirds of the mitre length.*

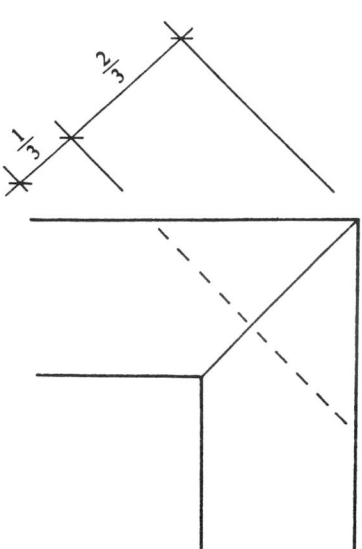

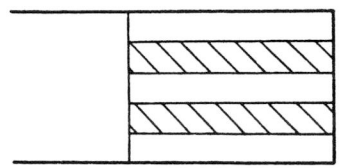

Diagram 97 *The mortise gauge is used to mark in the socket working from both edges.*

Diagram 98 *Place the frame in the vice with the shoulder line in the horizontal position.*

The shoulder of each socket is set in by two-thirds of the mitre length and at right angles to it (*diagram 96*). The sockets are scribed in, with the mortise gauge working from both edges to give a symmetrical joint (*diagram 97*).

The cutting of the sockets is made easier by placing the frame in the vice with the shoulder placed horizontally (*diagram 98*). Most of the waste is taken out with the coping saw and trimmed back with a mortise chisel, working from

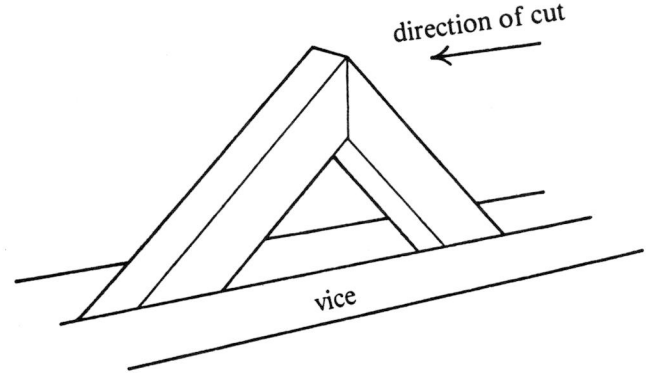

both sides. Because the joint has a long internal shoulder, its cutting may result in a slightly raised surface which will prevent the spline bedding down properly on the outside (*diagram 99*). Further removal of timber is necessary and, if

46

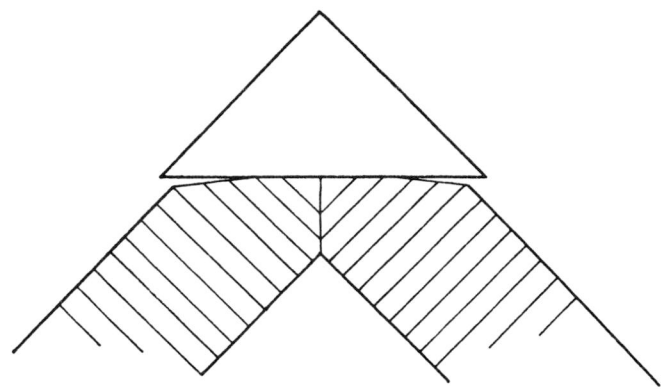

Diagram 99 *A badly cut shoulder prevents the spline bedding down on the outside.*

true flatness is difficult to achieve, it is preferable to have it slightly hollow (*diagram 100*).

Diagram 100 *A slightly hollow shoulder can be cut if a true flatness cannot be achieved.*

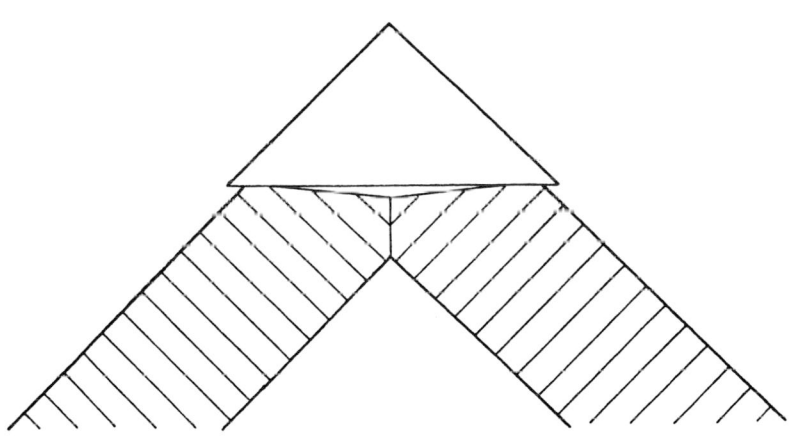

Splines are made to fit the socket with a push fit and can be planed flush after gluing. Alternatively they can be left proud, in which case a protrusion of about 3mm (⅛in.) is left with all corners rounded.

The construction of the joint can be further reflected and visually extended around the frame, by gluing strips of timber with the same thickness as the splines to both sides of each rail prior to construction (*diagram 101* and *figure 7*).

Diagram 101 *A contrasting strip of timber glued on to each edge improves visual quality.*

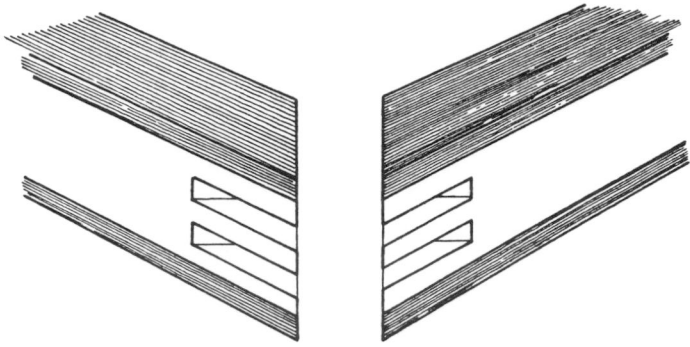

Figure 7 *Variation of splined mitre*

Square butt with contrasting inserts

A similar type of joint using the same method of construction replaces the mitre with a square butt and is built in the same manner as the standard bridle joint (*diagram 102* and *figure 8*).

Diagram 102 *Contrasting splines used in conjunction with a square butt.*

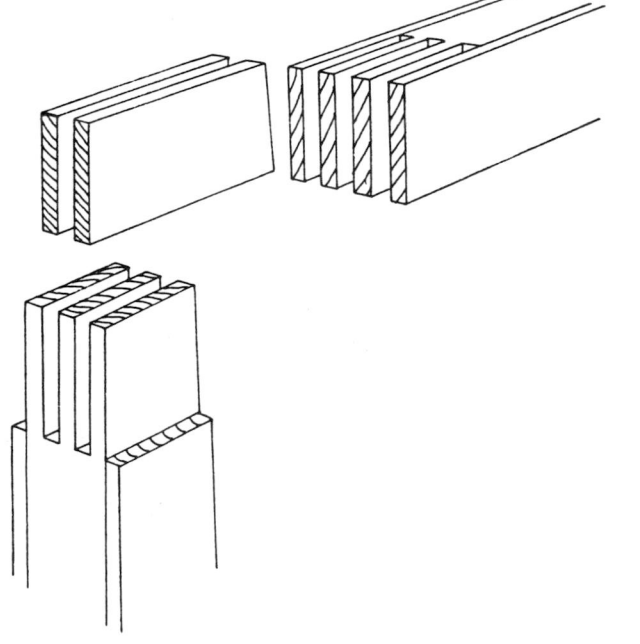

Figure 8 *Square butt and contrasting slip, similar to the bridle joint.*

The tenons are made in a contrasting timber and built into a rail. These should be twice as long as the rail width and should be set in by one-half of it (*diagram 103*). The sockets that accept them are identical for adjacent rails and should be marked together (*diagram 104*). The splines should be set into the sockets of one rail, and left protruding on both edges, to be planed flush after gluing. The two components should now go together.

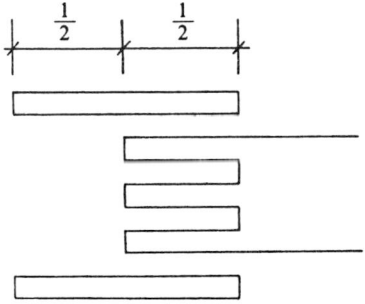

Diagram 103 *The spline is twice as long as the mortise.*

Diagram 104 *The inside shoulders of adjacent components can be marked together.*

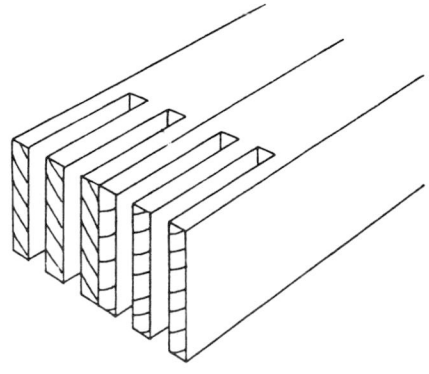

The two previous examples can be varied further by using a number of staggered inserts (*diagram 105* and *figure 9*). Joints of this type create great visual interest using a simple construction that is particularly strong due to the large gluing area.

Diagram 105 *Variation in spline length creates further interest.*

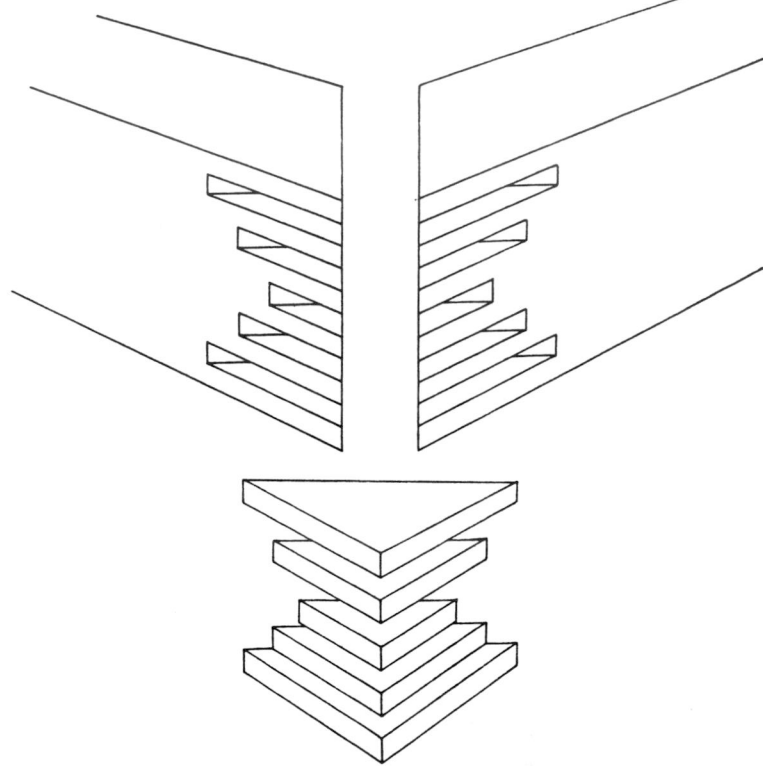

Figure 9 *Mitre and staggered inserts.*

3 Carcase Joinery

DECORATIVE DOVETAIL JOINTS

The traditional joint used in the construction of a carcase is the dovetail, primarily because it provides the strongest method of connecting two boards. Of the three main types of dovetail – through, lapped and secret – the through method provides the greatest visual interest because of the contrast between end and side grain emphasized in the proportions of pin to tail (*diagram 106* and *figure 10*). The strongest joint has

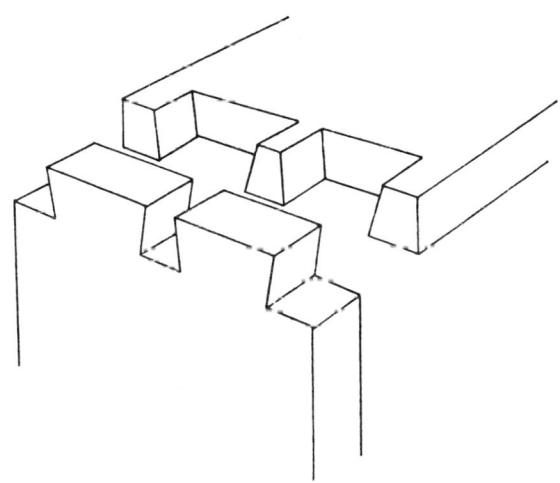

Diagram 106 *Standard through dovetail joint.*

Figure 10 *Through dovetail joint.*

both pins and tails of equal dimension, although a compromise is usually reached between strength and proportion by making the tails about twice the width of the pins at the shoulder (*diagram 107*).

Through dovetail
The pins are cut first, which will allow the tails to be marked easily; the sockets for the pins are usually too small to allow

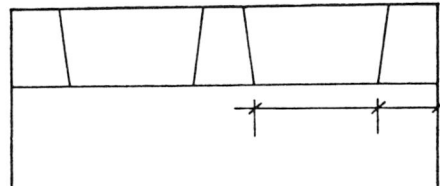

Diagram 107 *The pins and half pins are half the width of the tails at the inside shoulder.*

51

access for a pencil. The first step is to scribe the inside shoulder, which is measured in from the end of the board. This dimension should be the thickness of the board plus 1.5mm ($^1/_{16}$in.), which allows for any necessary planing down after construction. This is done lightly either with a knife and try-square working from the face side and face edge, or using a cutting gauge against the square end of the board. The depth of the lines can be increased in the waste areas after marking out the pins.

The width of pin and half pin are equal at the widest point, with the tail twice this width at its narrowest. Having decided the number of pins to use, divide the shoulder line up on the face side, which should be the inside of the carcase (*diagram 108*). These divisions are then drawn in from the inside shoulder to the end using a pencil and try-square.

The angle of the tail will depend on the type of work being undertaken and the timber being used for it. The usual practice is to have a steeper angle of about 1:5 in softer materials and for work where appearance is not important and an angle of about 1:8 for finer jointing (*diagram 109*). It is up to the individual to select the correct angle for a particular job, but he should be aware that a sharp angle will result in weak, short grain at the extremity of the tail, while a shallow angle will reduce mechanical efficiency. When the

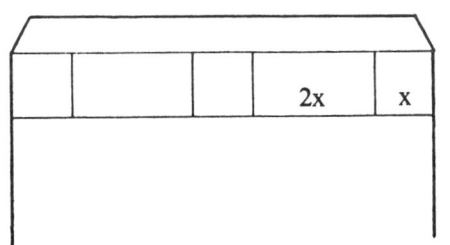

Diagram 108   *The joint is divided up on the face side*

Diagram 109   *The angle of the dovetail can vary between 1:5 and 1:8 depending on use and material.*

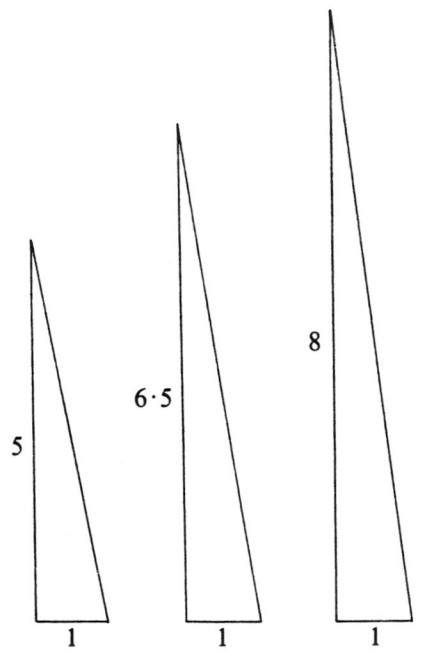

angle is established, set it on a sliding bevel and pencil in the lines of the end grain (*diagram 110*). The marking of the tail is then completed by taking the lines from the end to the inside shoulder and shading all the waste area to denote its removal. An alternative method of marking the joint is to make a number of dovetail templates at varying angles and select one for a specific purpose.

Place the board vertically in the vice and, using a fine dovetail saw, make cuts on the waste side of the lines down to the shoulder. Make sure the saw blade is kept in the vertical position, only cutting into the waste, as any deviation may be visible in the finished joint. A coping saw is used to remove most of the waste; work its blade down the vertical sawcut and gradually bring it into the horizontal position close to the shoulder line, leaving about 1mm (1/32in.) of waste (*diagram 111*). The advantage of distinct knife lines is illustrated at

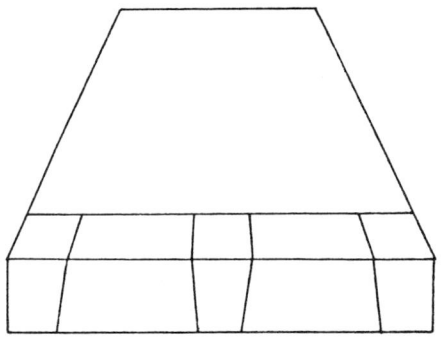

Diagram 110 *The sliding bevel and pencil are used to mark the angle on the end grain.*

Diagram 111 *Most of the waste is removed with the coping saw.*

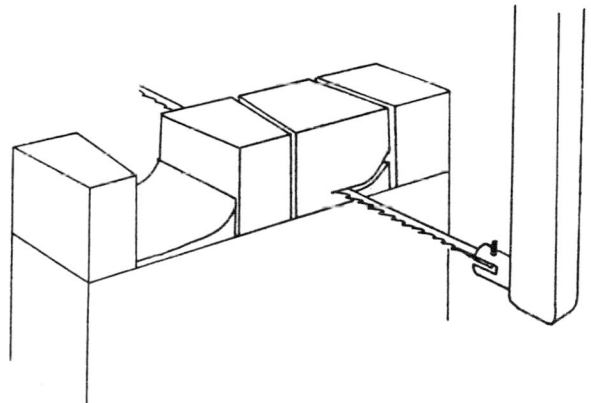

this point, the location of the paring chisel being made easy when removing the waste (*diagram 112*). The chisel should be kept at right angles to the board, cutting from both sides

Diagram 112 *The paring chisel is used to cut back to the shoulder.*

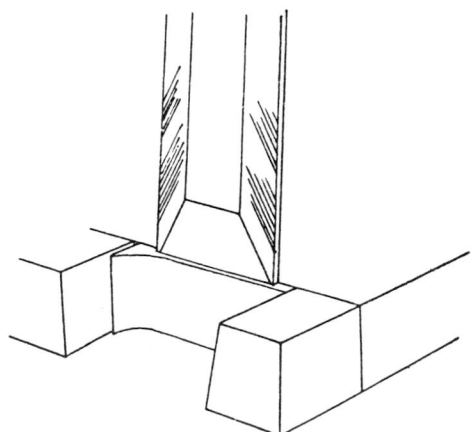

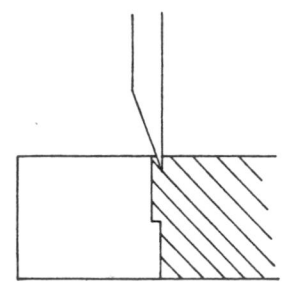

Diagram 113   *Waste is removed from both sides.*

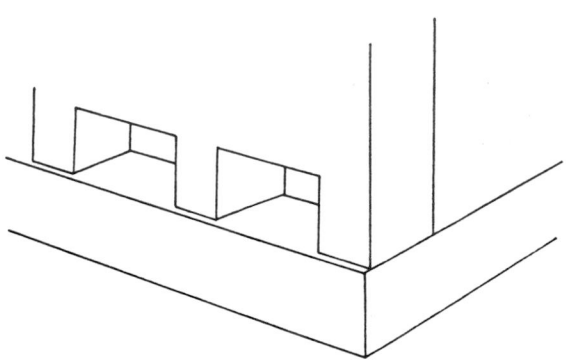

Diagram 114   *Use the pins as a template to mark in the tails.*

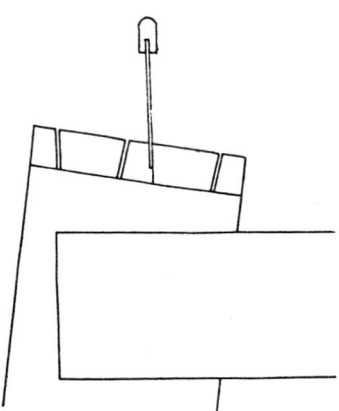

Diagram 116   *The panel is placed in the vice so that sawcuts are made vertically.*

Diagram 117   *Any protrusion will prevent joint assembly.*

to prevent timber break-out (*diagram 113*). Any remaining waste on the tails should also be taken back to the lines with a paring chisel.

When complete, the pins are used as a template to mark out the tails on the adjacent panel. The boards are held at right angles, with the inside of the pins resting on the shoulder line and each face edge being flush (*diagram 114*). If the boards are large, some method of holding them steady should be found, such as cramping them lightly to the bench. The tails can then be marked in with pencil (*diagram 115*).

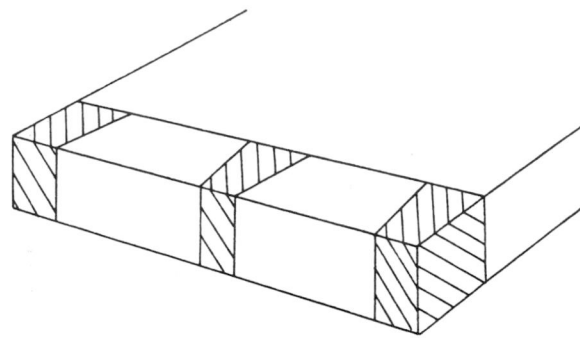

Diagram 115   *Shaded areas denote waste.*

The cutting of the tails follows the same process as the pins, but to assist accurate cutting, place the outline of the tail in a vertical position when securing it in the vice (*diagram 116*). When cutting back to the shoulder, select a chisel that is slightly narrower than the width of the socket, and work from both sides. If the joint has been cut accurately it should go together with a few taps of the hammer (use scrap material to prevent bruising of the panels). Problems may occur if the shoulders have not been cut accurately, a common fault being to leave a protrusion at the centre of the shoulder which obviously prevents the joint going together on the outside (*diagram 117*). It may be preferable to have a slight hollow on

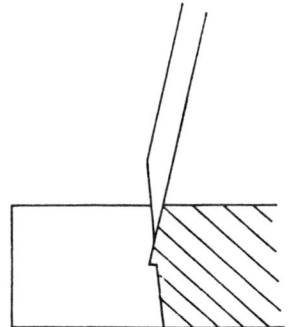

the shoulder which should be made when the waste is removed. This is done by paring down vertically for one-quarter of the thickness and then tilting the chisel forward slightly and cutting to the middle. The panel is then reversed and the operation repeated (*diagram 118*). Another fault is to leave waste material in the corners of the sockets, which again prevents the joint going together, and this should be removed.

Dovetail joint with intermediate pins

Variations of the dovetail joint often create further visual interest. By introducing intermediate pins into the main tails the decorative quality of the joint is considerably increased and this has the added advantage of providing additional strength where it is needed, i.e. at the centre of a wide tail (*diagram 119* and *figure 11*). As visual quality is of great importance, marking out must be accurate, with neat cutting of both pins and tails, and so the use of this method on thin boards is inadvisable.

Preparation of the boards is virtually the same as for the through dovetail up to the marking out stage, but should

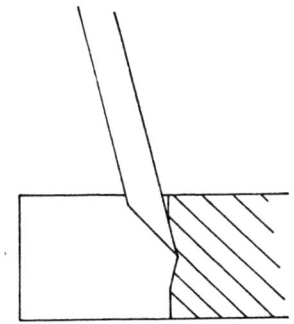

Diagram 118 *The hollow shoulder can be used.*

Diagram 119 *Decorative dovetail joint.*

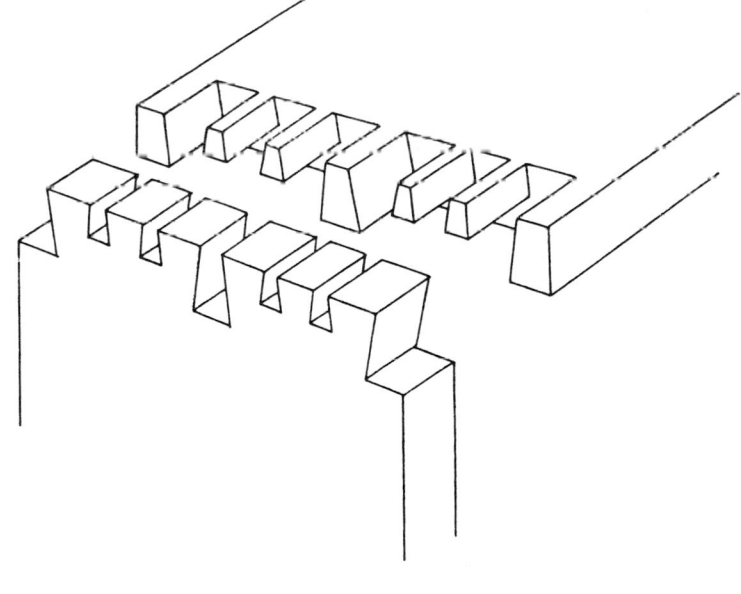

Figure 11 *Decorative dovetail joint.*

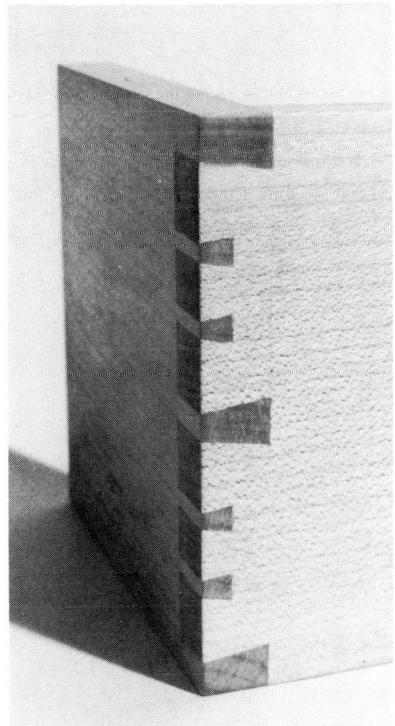

include the inside shoulder of the small pins which is one-half the board thickness measured from the main shoulder line (*diagram 120*). Because of the introduction of small pins, a wider tail must be used in order to accommodate them. Their

Diagram 120 *The shoulders of the small pins have to be marked.*

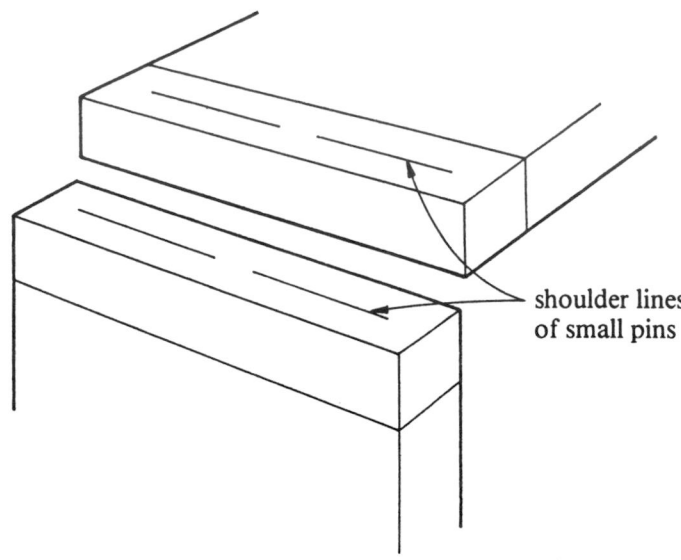

shoulder lines
of small pins

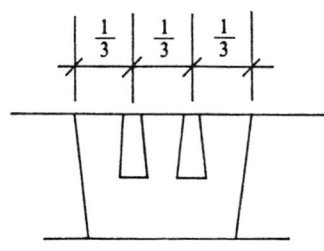

Diagram 121 *Small pins are set symmetrically through the tail.*

Diagram 122 *The inside half of the waste is initially removed.*

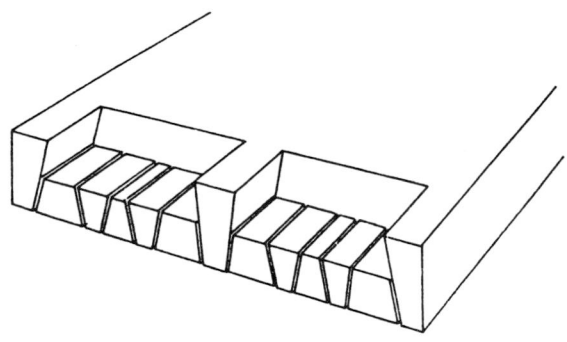

centres are found by dividing the tail into three equal parts at its widest (*diagram 121*).

Waste areas are again shaded and vertical sawcuts made on the waste side of the lines. The inside half of waste must be removed completely and this should be done by chopping from the top end while the board is secured to a solid worktop (*diagram 122*). The remaining waste can mostly be taken out with a coping saw and trimmed back to the shoulder. A waste block equal to one-half the board thickness should be inserted to prevent the timber splitting (*diagram 123*).

Sawing the tails follows the same procedure as a standard dovetail, setting the board in the vice with the marked lines in a vertical position. To assist location of the joint, the internal corners of the tails can be slightly relieved (*diagram 124*).

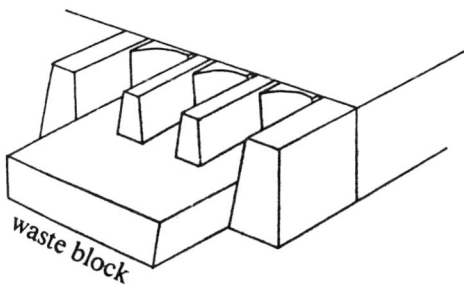

Diagram 123 *A waste block prevents the timber splitting.*

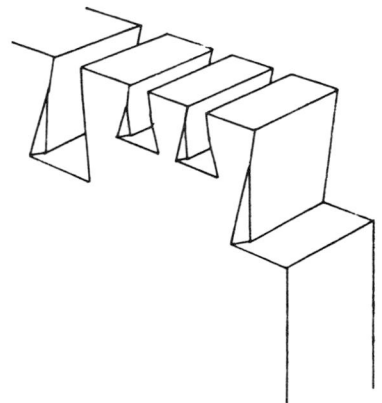

Diagram 124 *Inside corners can be removed to assist assembly.*

Dovetail joint with contrasting tails
The problem with the previously mentioned dovetail joints is that they are visually confined to the corner in the carcase. A variation that overcomes this uses the insertion of contrasting components to create the tails of the joint (*diagram 125* and

Diagram 125 *Contrasting inserts create the tails.*

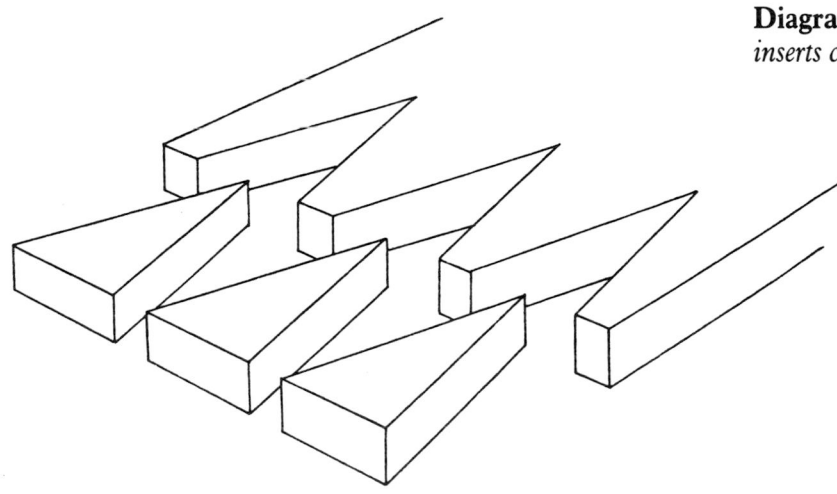

Figure 12 *V-shaped inserts create the tail in the joint.*

figure 12). These are made approximately 3mm (⅛in.) thicker than the boards they are to be set into and have an internal angle of 30°. Their ends can either be rounded to any convenient diameter or left pointed, although the latter may cause difficulty when cutting the internal angle of the socket.

The number of inserts will depend on the width of the panel, and should be shaped with all square edges, as any deviation will result in a badly fitting joint. The panels they are to be set into should be prepared with square ends and a length equal to the internal dimension of the finished carcase.

To mark out the sockets, use each insert as a template set onto the board and spaced at regular intervals (*diagram 126*).

Diagram 126 *Each insert is used as a template to mark the outline of each socket.*

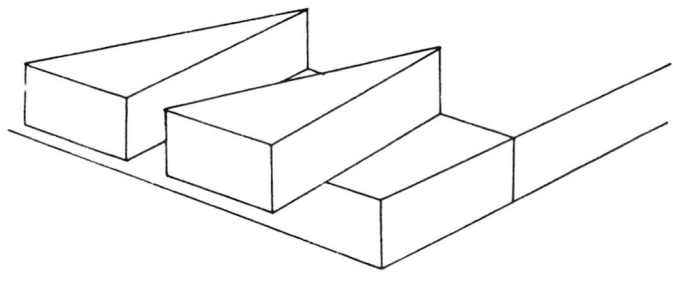

If a rounded end is preferred, drill holes through the board and set the inserts on top of them. A knife is then used to mark in the sockets. To assist their location, draw in centre lines to correspond to those on the panel (*diagram 127*).

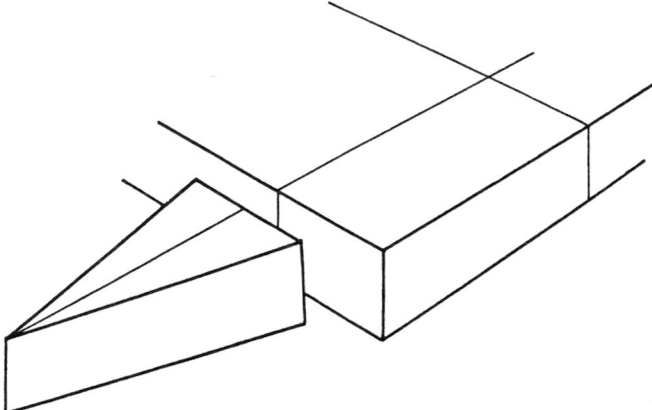

Diagram 127 *Centre lines help locate the insert on the board.*

The type of saw that is used to remove the waste will depend on the length of cut. Since dovetail and tenon saws are restricted, a panel saw or even a Japanese Ryoba saw should be employed. Cutting on the waste side of the line, saw down to the internal corner or pre-cut hole on both sides to create the socket. Any deviation of the blade into the waste can be trimmed with a chisel, but if the cut goes beyond the socket line then a blemish in the final joint will result.

Fit and glue the inserts into their corresponding sockets, each one slightly protruding on both sides of the panel. These can then be planed flush to the panel when the glue is set (*diagram 128*).

The tailed panel is used to mark the adjoining pins in a

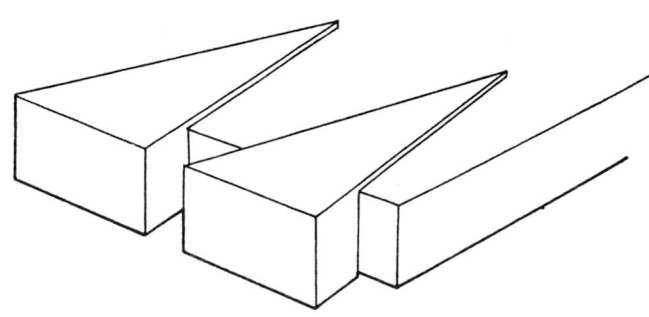

Diagram 128 *Any protrusion of the insert is planed flush after the glue has set.*

similar manner to the standard dovetails, the process being reversed on this occasion.

Variations on this theme can be achieved in a number of ways. Inlaid strips can be used to link up the tails on opposite corners (*diagram 129* and *figure 13*) or the adjoining panel can be made of the same type of timber as the inserts.

Diagram 129   *Inlayed strips of veneer visually extend the joint from corner to corner.*

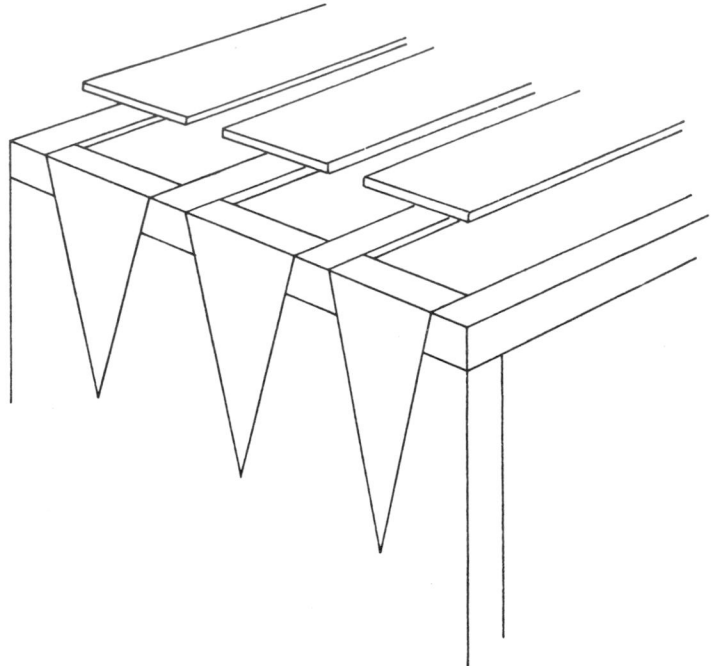

Figure 13   *Inlayed strips link up opposite corners.*

Alternatively, the length of each insert can vary, which will in turn vary the width of tails. If each insert lengthens towards the centre of the panel, the tails are narrowest at the outer edge, thus giving additional strength where it is most needed (*diagram 130* and *figure 14*).

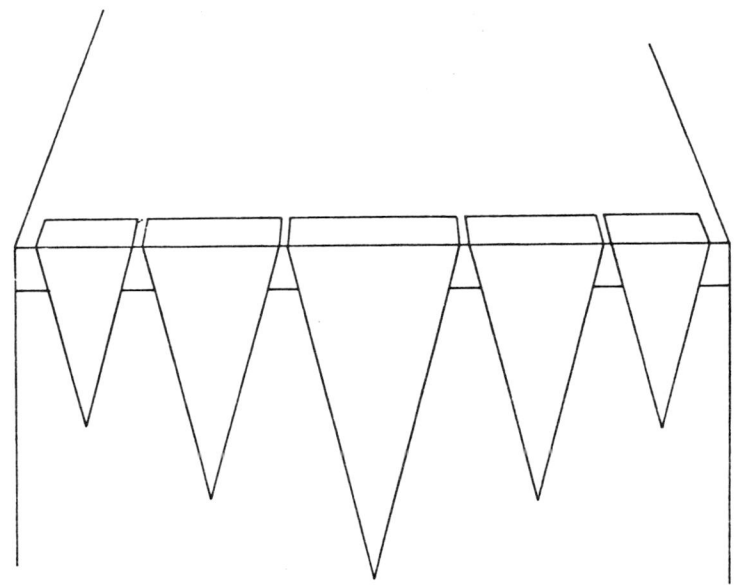

Diagram 130 *Variation in tail length creates further interest.*

Figure 14 *Variation of tail width.*

61

Butt mitre with dovetail key

The basic principle of locking two panels together by the use of a dovetail can be used to great visual effect when employing a shaped key in conjunction with the mitre (*diagram 131* and *figure 15*). The carcase must be constructed

Diagram 131   *The butt mitre used in conjunction with a dovetail.*

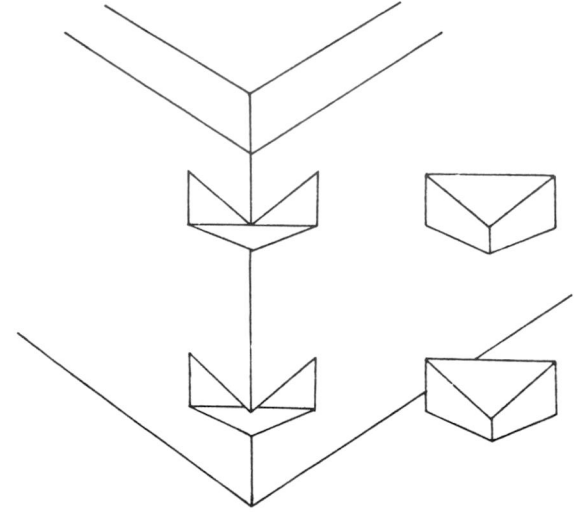

Figure 15   *Mitre and dovetail key.*

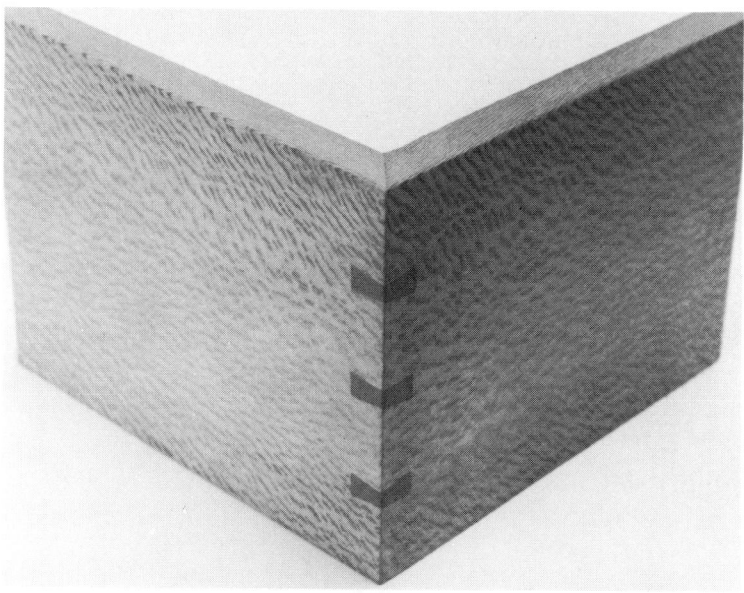

prior to inserting the dovetail keys and is made with a simple butt mitre cut on the donkey's ear (*diagram 132*). This can be virtually finished prior to cutting the sockets, but care must be taken as it may not withstand rough handling.

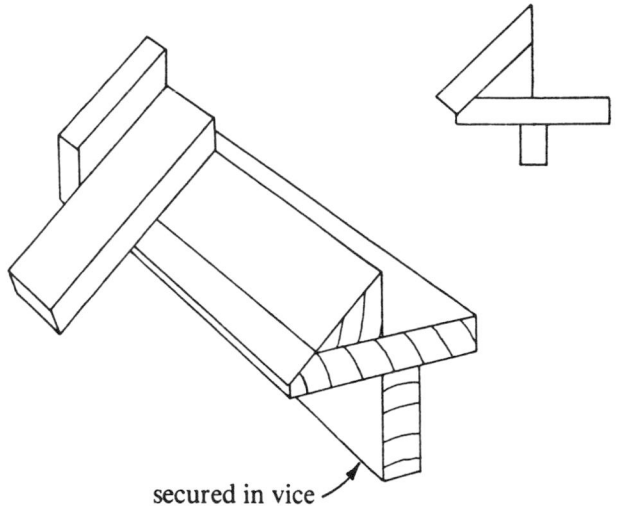

secured in vice

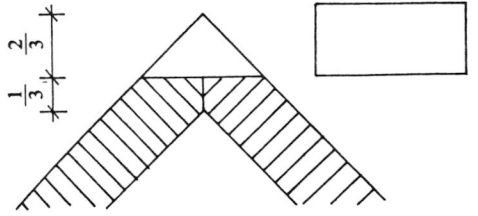

Diagram 132 *The donkey's ear.*

Diagram 133 *The shoulder is set in by two-thirds of the mitre length.*

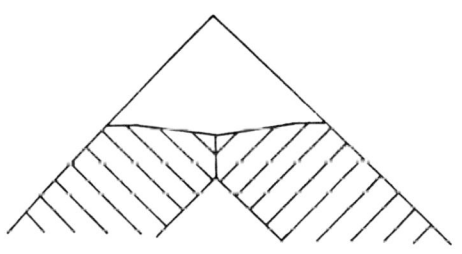

Diagram 134 *A hollow shoulder assists spline entry.*

To mark out the sockets, set a sliding bevel at an angle of 1:8 and pencil in the outline on both surfaces. At its narrowest part it should not exceed 3mm (⅛in.) and be finer if possible. The inside shoulder of the socket is set in by two-thirds of the mitre width and square to it (*diagram 133*).

Difficulty may be experienced when removing the waste in trying to keep the sawcut exactly to the line on both surfaces. Continual checking of the cut as the operation progresses is essential because subsequent trimming with a chisel is extremely difficult due to the narrow access available. Most of the waste is removed with a coping saw, and is trimmed back to the shoulder with a fine paring chisel to give a flat shoulder. Care should be taken to avoid any protrusions which may prevent the dovetail key slipping in easily. Entry is made easier by having a slightly hollow shoulder (*diagram 134*).

The keys are made by planing a long strip of timber to the correct angle and cutting it to the required lengths. To assist the shaping, two simple jigs are made in which to rest the timber (*diagram 135*). Each key is individually fitted until all

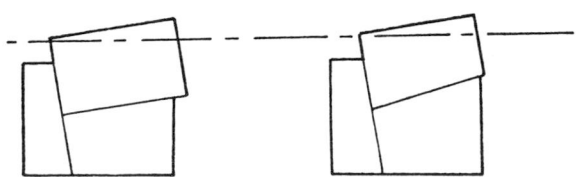

Diagram 135 *Two jigs are used to assist planing of the dovetail keys.*

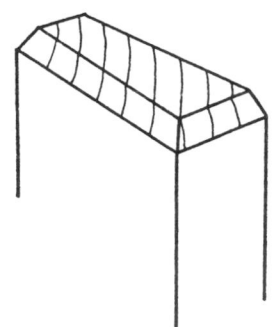

Diagram 136 *Chamfering each key will assist its entry.*

Diagram 137 *Excess timber is removed by planing with the grain of the key.*

are a hand-push fit, and they are then glued into position, one end being chamfered to assist entry (*diagram 136*). When the glue is set, excess timber is removed by planing with the grain of the keys (*diagram 137*).

direction of planing

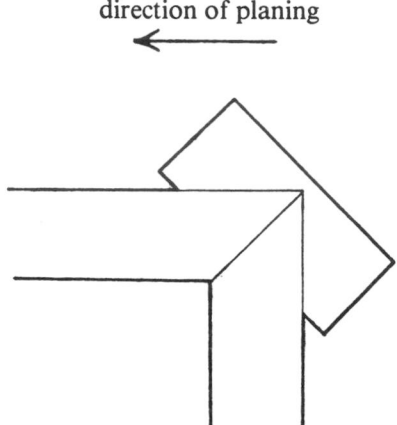

DECORATIVE FINGER (CORNER-LOCK) JOINTS

By replacing the dovetail with the finger (corner-lock) joint in a carcase construction, many more variations are possible. This usually provides additional strength as well as introducing contrasting members to highlight the structure.

Probably one of the most successful methods of increasing visual and structural quality was again a product of the Greene brothers, who enjoyed considerable success with its use. The strength of the finger joint is considerably increased by the introduction of contrasting pegs which lock the construction in both planes (*diagram 138* and *figure 16*).

Diagram 138 *The finger joint used in conjunction with contrasting dowels.*

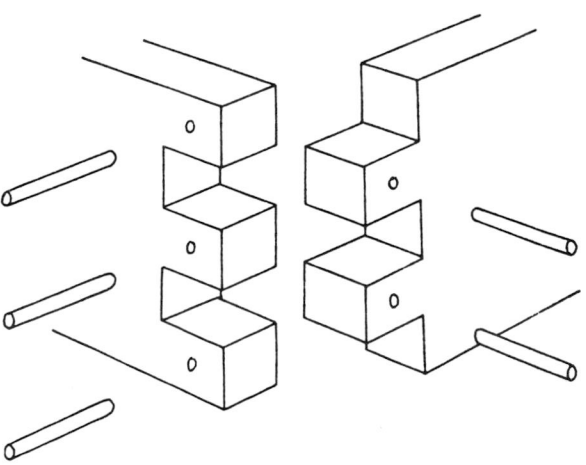

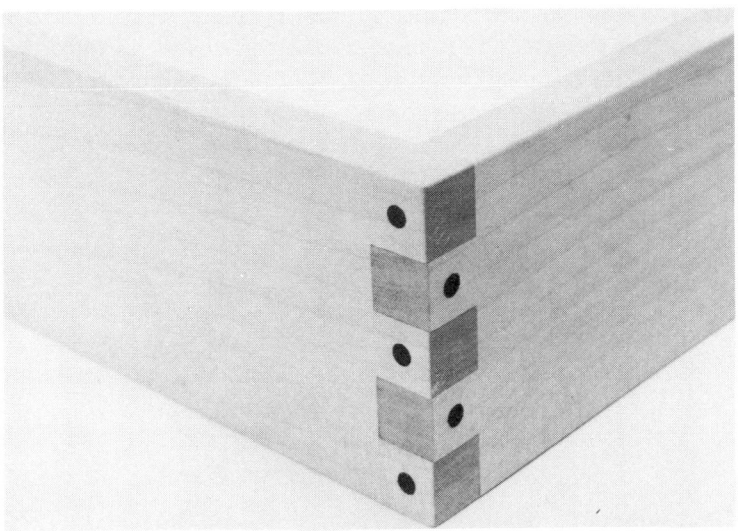

Figure 16 *Finger joint and contrasting pegs.*

With all timber prepared, opposite boards can be cramped together and the fingers marked by dividing their width up into an odd number of parts with equal dimensions (*diagram 139*). Separate the boards and take the lines from the end to the shoulder using a pencil and try-square (*diagram 140*).

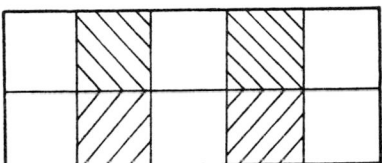

Diagram 139 *Opposite boards are marked together.*

Diagram 140 *Use a pencil and try-square to take the lines from the end to the shoulder.*

Diagram 141 *Waste areas should be shaded.*

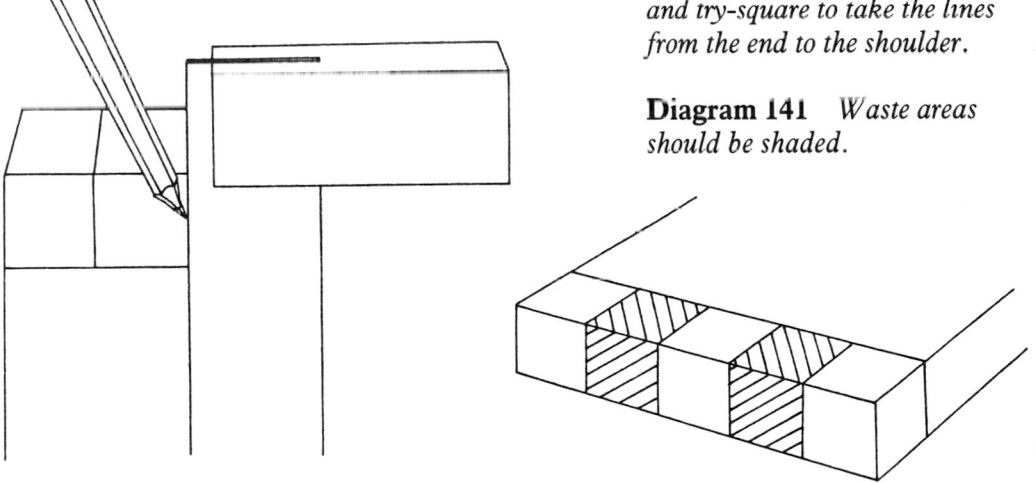

Shade all the waste areas and emphasize the shoulder line to assist location of the chisel (*diagram 141*).

Place the board in the vice with the fingers held vertically, and use a dovetail saw to make the cuts on the waste side of

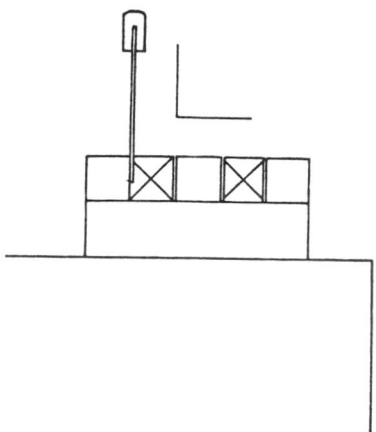

the line down to the shoulder (*diagram 142*). The process of removing the waste is the same as for the dovetail joint but made easier because of the square shoulders (*diagram 143*).

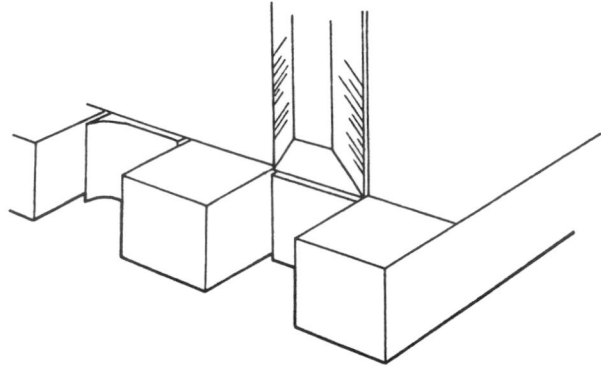

Diagram 142   *All sawcuts are made vertically.*

Diagram 143   *Waste is removed by a paring chisel.*

The finished fingers are used as a template to mark those on the adjoining board (*diagram 144*), and the cutting process is repeated. If the operations are carried out accurately, the joint will go together with a gentle tap of the hammer, using a piece of waste material on the panel to prevent bruising. To

Diagram 144   *The finished fingers of one panel are used as a template to mark those on the adjoining panel.*

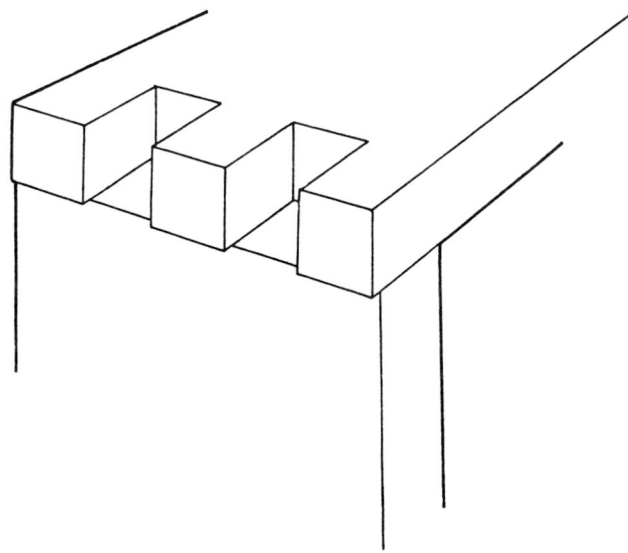

help it go together either remove the internal corners, or slightly chamfer the waste at the end of the fingers (*diagram 145*). The carcase is glued together with the aid of cramping blocks that give pressure only where needed, pushing each

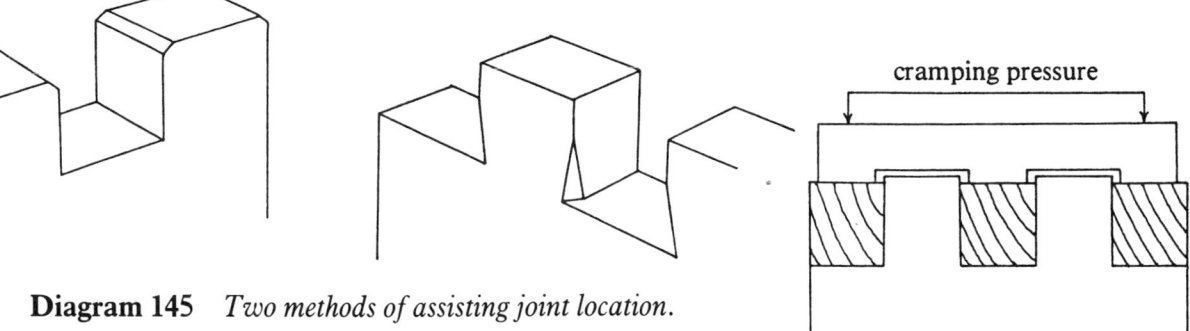

Diagram 145 *Two methods of assisting joint location.*

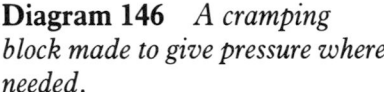

finger against the inside shoulder (*diagram 146*). After the glue has set, the protruding waste can be planed away leaving a flush joint. To prevent the end grain splitting, the corner of each finger is removed on the inside (*diagram 147*).

The joint is now ready to accept the pegs. Each hole is drilled at the centre of the finger using a brad-point drill which will give a positive location and clean cut (*diagram 148*). If a square hole is needed, the round hole is squared off

Diagram 146 *A cramping block made to give pressure where needed.*

direction of planing
→

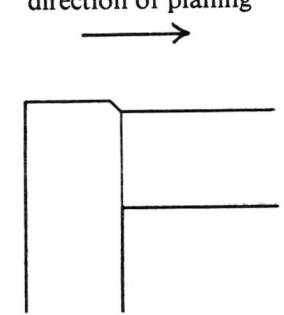

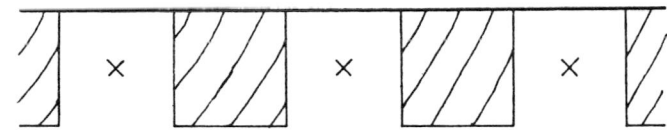

Diagram 148 *The centres of the holes are marked in a symmetrical position.*

Diagram 147 *The removal of the internal corner prevents the timber splitting.*

Diagram 150 *A space between the bottom of the hole and the end of the peg takes up excess glue.*

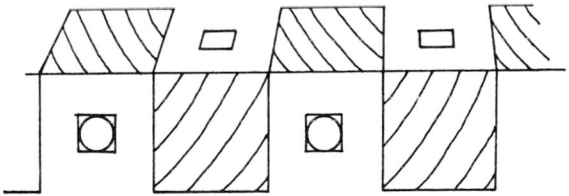

Diagram 149 *Round holes are squared off to receive a square peg.*

to accept the corresponding peg (*diagram 149*). When gluing in the peg, allow a small airspace at the bottom of the hole to take up any excess glue which will otherwise have nowhere to escape and may cause the timber to split (*diagram 150*). Many variations of this joint are possible and the Greenes incorporated many examples in their work. The width of the

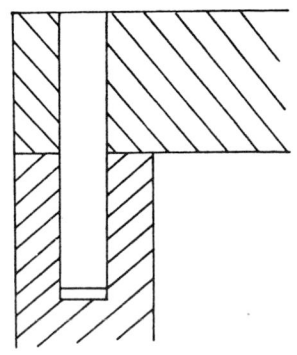

finger can be varied with the corresponding number of pegs in it increased (*diagram 151, figure 17*).

Ideally, the perfect decorative joint should extend beyond the confines of the corner and become a major visual element in a design that continually draws the eye back to the method of construction. This is successfully achieved by building up the panels from strips of contrasting timber. This method will also give a perfectly fitting joint if the process is carried out accurately prior to laminating the strips.

Diagram 151 *Variation of finger width and number of dowels.*

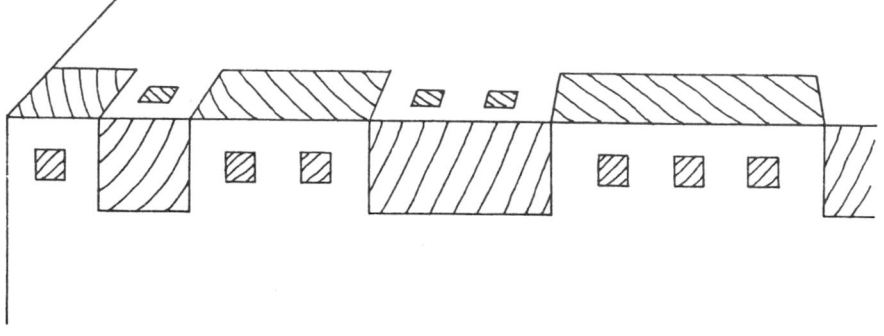

Figure 17 *Variation in finger width and corresponding number of pegs.*

Finger joints with contrasting panels

The first example in this range introduces a contrasting veneer between each strip (*diagram 152, figure 18*). To make it, begin by veneering both sides of a wide board to produce the strip in the panel. The thickness of this board, including the veneer combination, will be the width of the laminated fingers in the joint and is therefore an important dimension. If the joint is to be used on a large structure, it may be advisable to purchase panels that have been accurately

Diagram 152 *A contrasting veneer provides decoration.*

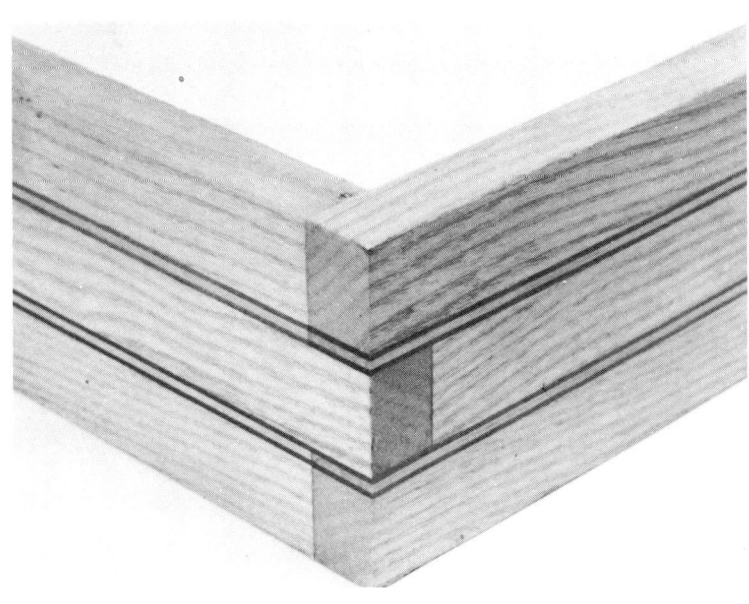

Figure 18 *Contrasting veneer used in the finger joint.*

planed by machine. This, and an unveneered board, is cut into strips, their width being slightly larger than the thickness of the finished panels. Their ends are planed square at alternate lengths; the shorter ones determine the inside dimension of each side of the finished carcase and the long ones are slightly greater than the outside dimension.

When all the strips have been prepared, a simple jig is required to glue up the panel which will locate the inside shoulder of the joint (*diagram 153*). Two through housings

Diagram 153 *The jig used to locate the strips in the panel.*

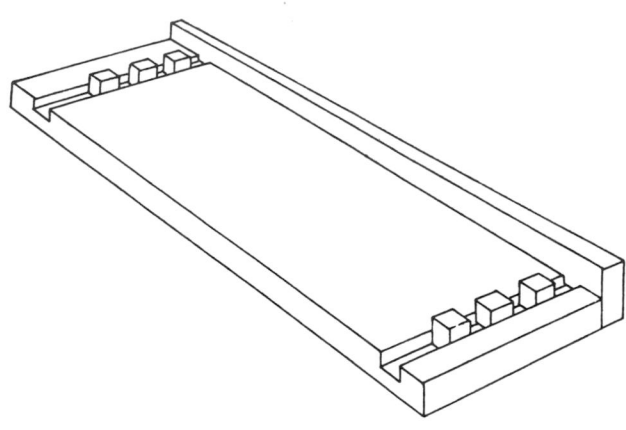

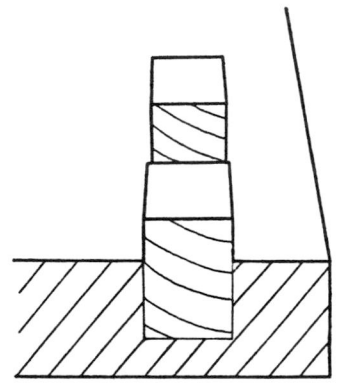

Diagram 154 *Inserted stops used to locate inside shoulders.*

are cut on a flat board (plywood, chipboard, etc.) into which are pressed pieces of timber to form the stops (*diagram 154*).

Difficulty may be experienced when cramping the strips together if movement occurs, as this could result in a bowed panel. This is overcome by placing blocks of timber across the panel's width, which are then cramped to the jig (*diagram 155*). These blocks and the jig should be pre-waxed to prevent their adhesion to the panel. When the glue is set, take the panels out of the jig and lightly plane both sides prior to constructing the carcase. If the original boards were accurately planed, the joint should fit perfectly.

Diagram 155 *Blocks of timber prevent cupping of the panel.*

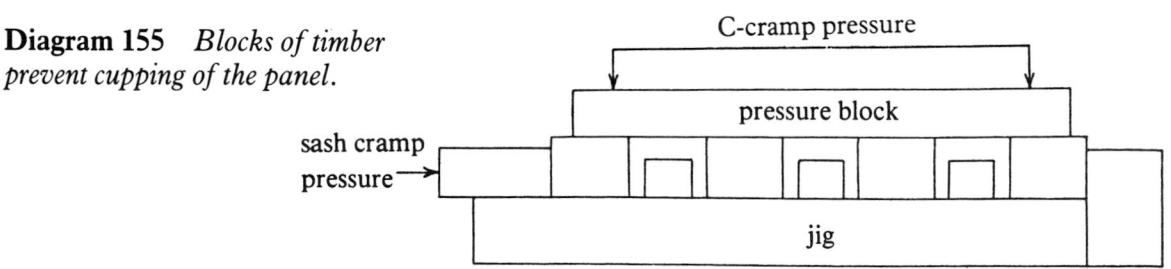

This method of construction offers great scope for a wide variety of decorative joinery. The strips can be made of contrasting timber to form another simple decorative effect (*diagram 156, figure 19*), or developed further by varying their width, increasing in size towards the centre of the panel (*diagram 157, figure 20*). Each of these joints can be formed

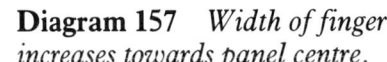

Diagram 156 *Strips can be made in contrasting timber.*

Figure 19 *Finger joint using contrasting strips of timber.*

Figure 20 *A joint using varying finger widths.*

Diagram 157 *Width of finger increases towards panel centre.*

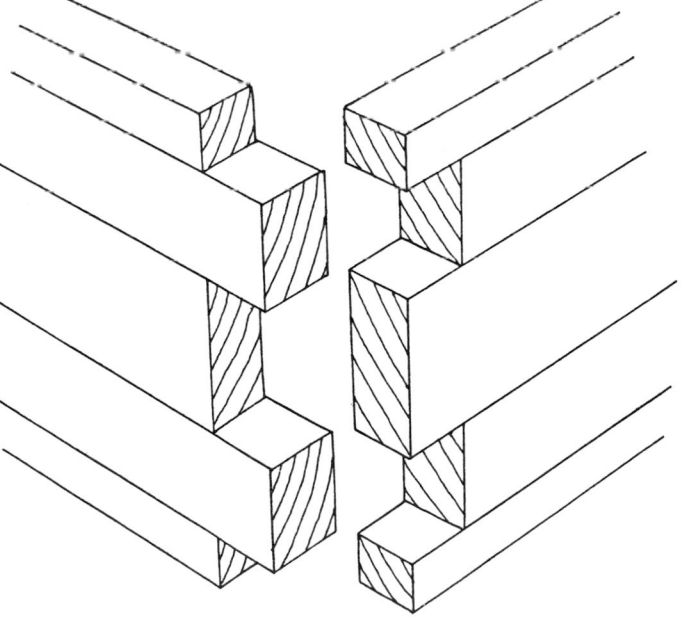

Figure 21 *Three-way corner using a finger joint.*

into a three-way corner by using a mitre to join two surfaces (*figure 21*).

Finger-joint with V-shaped inserts

A further example of a decorative finger joint has panels that are constructed in a completely different manner to previous examples (*diagram 158, figure 22*). Cut the timber to the required length, width and thickness. The length will form the inside dimension of the carcase, the width is twice that of the finger in the joint (*diagram 159*), and the thickness should be slightly greater than the finished panel size.

The mitred corners require great accuracy if the joint is to function efficiently and should be cut using either a guillotine or a mitre shooting board (*see diagram 62, p. 30*). The contrasting fingers should also be cut in this way.

Each panel is glued together with the aid of a jig similar to that in diagram 154, leaving out the two components that form the front and back edges. This allows a through groove to be cut on the end of each panel that will accept the plywood spline (*diagram 160*). This is cut with a plough plane and the panel then finished by gluing on the remaining components. The groove is extended into these components by removing the waste with a mortise chisel of equal dimension. A similar

1 Jewellery casket in French walnut
   and sycamore

2 Jewellery casket open

3 Triangular box in yew and walnut with cedar lining

4 Low tables in rosewood/yew and black bean/sycamore

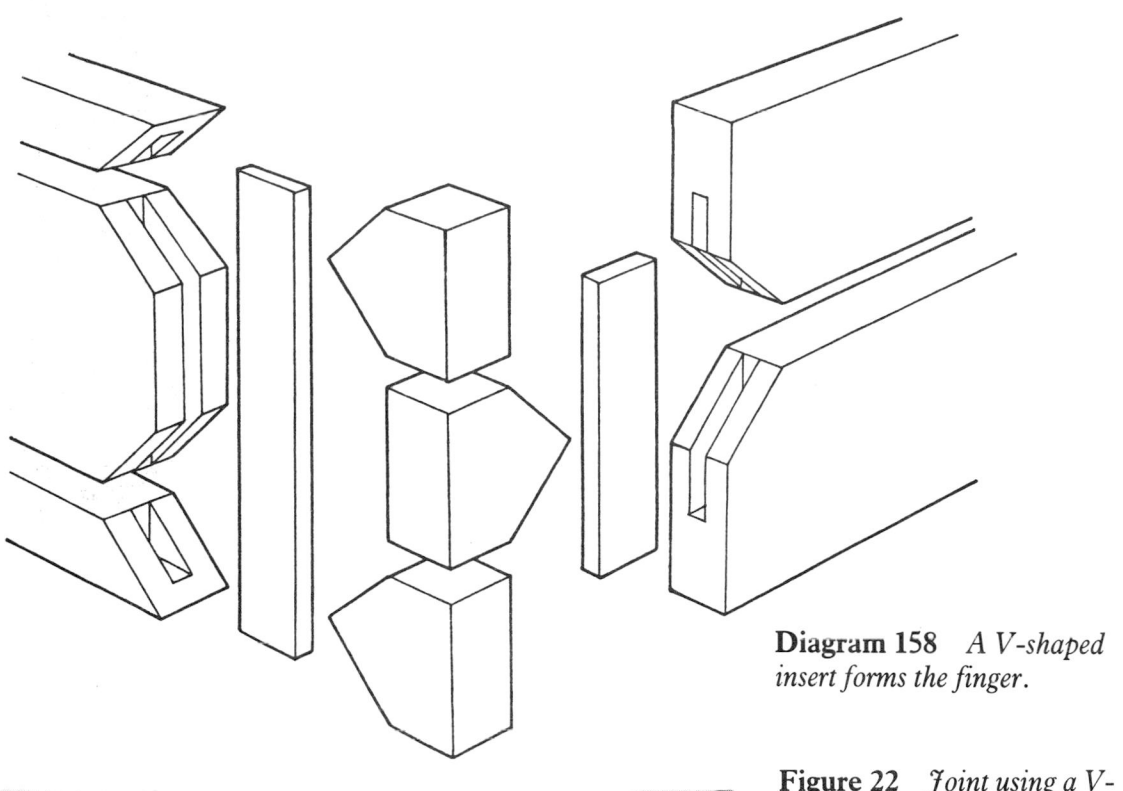

Diagram 158   *A V-shaped insert forms the finger.*

Figure 22   *Joint using a V-shaped finger insert.*

Diagram 159   *Each component is twice the finger width.*

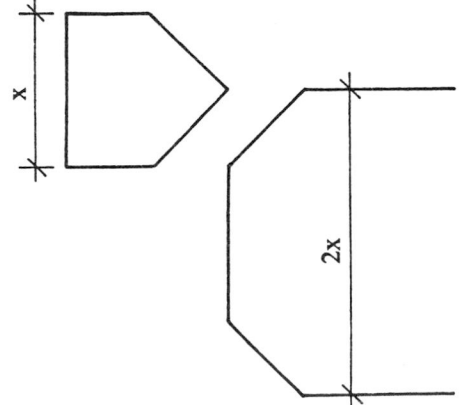

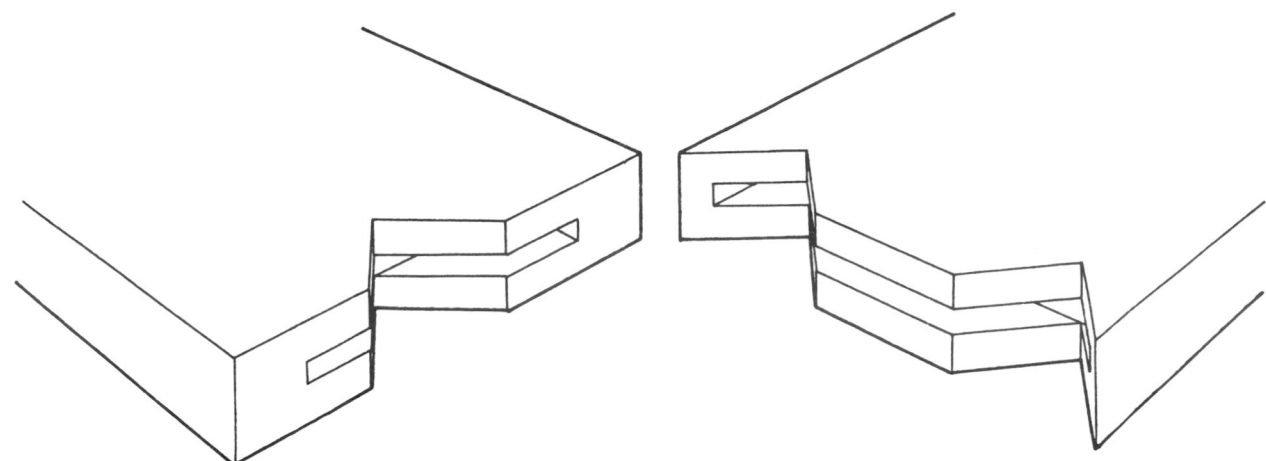

Diagram 160 *A groove in the end grain accepts the plywood spline.*

groove is cut into the end of each finger insert. The panels are then completed by gluing each finger into its respective recess in the panel. Finally, lightly plane each side of the panel to remove any discrepancy, and glue the carcase together.

In an effort to extend the joint visually around the carcase, strips of veneer can be applied to the edge of each component prior to removing the corners. This will result in a series of fine lines connecting the points of the contrasting finger inserts (*diagram 161, figure 23*).

Figure 23 *Variation on figure 22.*

Diagram 161 *Additional interest is created by veneering the edge of each component.*

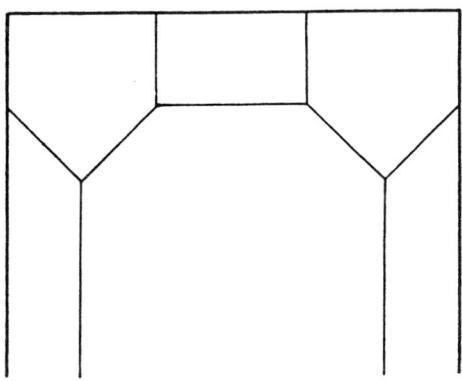

DECORATIVE MITRE JOINTS

The use of the butt mitre together with a strengthening insert has been illustrated when discussing the dovetail joint (*see diagram 131, p. 62*). The mitre, although not usually thought strong enough to be the sole method of corner fastening, offers the foundation for many visually interesting joints when used with other contrasting components.

Mitre joint with contrasting strips

The insertion of thin strips of timber running from corner to corner shows one simple method of adding strength while leading the eye around the carcase to the decorative corners (*diagram 162* and *figure 24*).

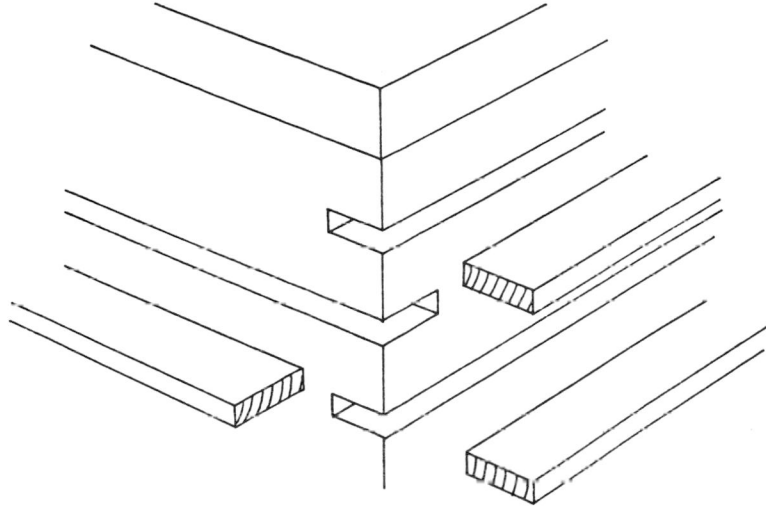

Diagram 162 *Thin strips of timber set into a mitre create additional strength.*

Figure 24 *Mitre and strip inserts.*

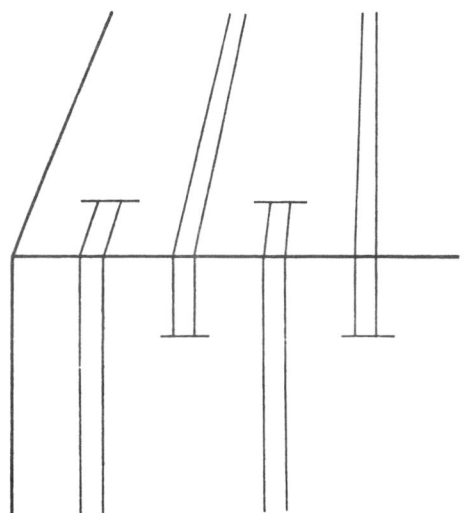

Starting with a mitred carcase, determine the number and position of strips to be used. Select a plough plane blade of appropriate width and set the points of a mortice gauge to it. Adjusting the fence of the gauge when necessary, scribe in the position of each strip, working from both edges of the panel (*diagram 163*). The depth of each slot is marked in with a cutting gauge, with the parallel lines scribed up to it. Prior to cutting the grooves, waste should be removed at the corners to prevent timber splitting as the blade runs through the end (*diagram 164*).

Diagram 163   *The position of each slot is scribed with the marking gauge.*

Diagram 164   *Waste is removed at one end to prevent break-out as the plane blade emerges.*

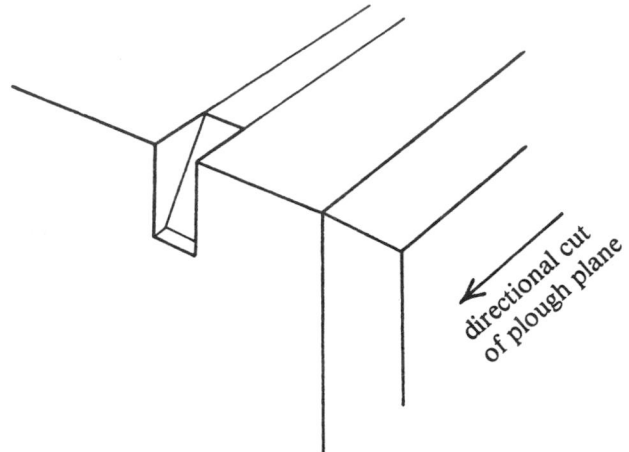

directional cut of plough plane

With all the slots cut to the correct depth, contrasting strips of timber are planed to the same dimension. Working on opposite panels in each operation, apply glue to the slots and insert the strips, exerting pressure at the corners to ensure that they bed down accurately (*diagram 165*). When the glue is set, the strips are planed flush to the panel and the operation repeated on the two remaining surfaces.

Diagram 165   *Cramping blocks are used to bed down each strip accurately.*

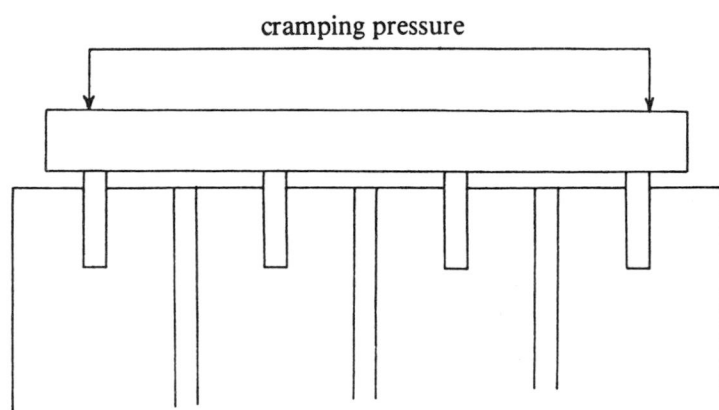

cramping pressure

An alternative method of using these strips would be to terminate them a short way into the carcase in which case the stopped grooves would have to be chopped out with a mortise chisel (*diagram 166* and *figure 25*). Further visual

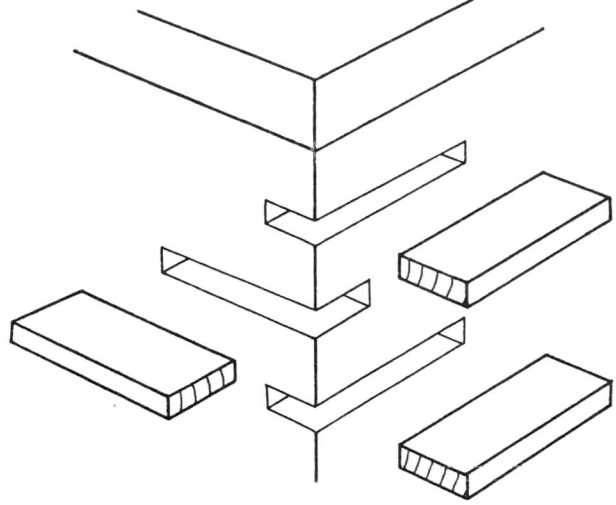

Diagram 166   *Short strips of timber can also be used.*

Figure 25   *Mitre and stopped-strip inserts.*

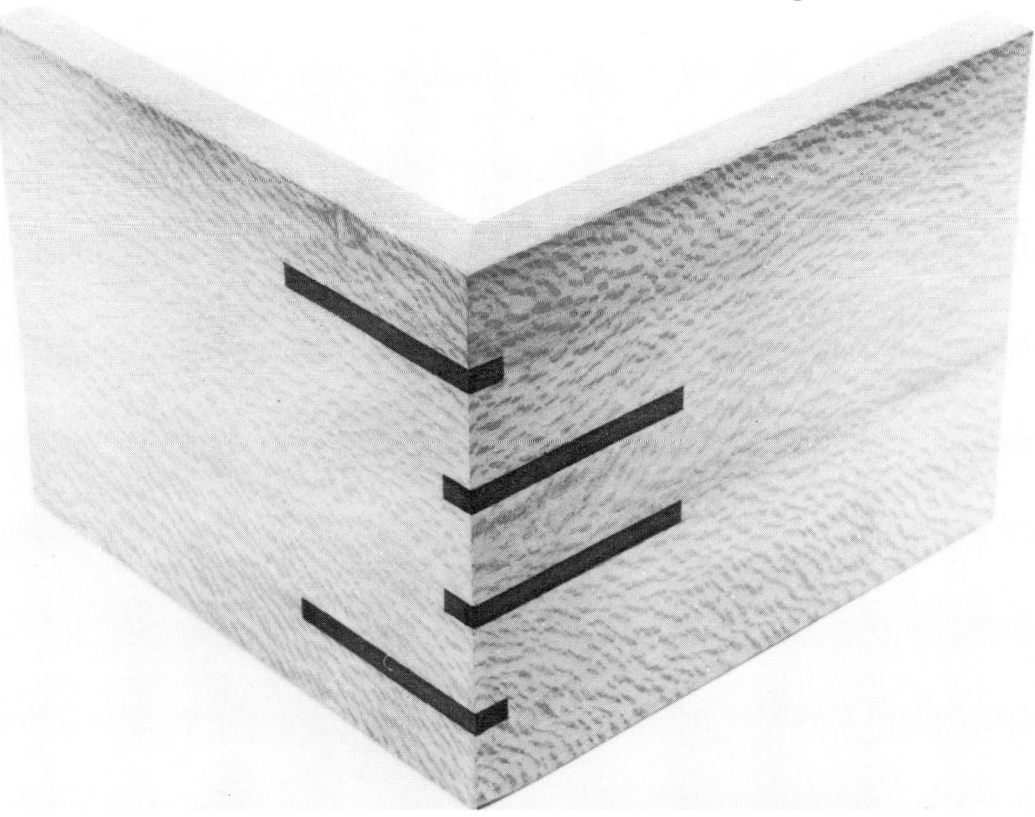

improvement of this example is achieved by joining the ends of the strips across the grain (*diagram 167* and *figure 26*).

Occasionally, certain parts of different joints can be combined to create new decorative constructions. A combination of the strips used in the previous example and

Diagram 167 *Visual quality is improved by joining up the ends of the strips with a veneer inlay.*

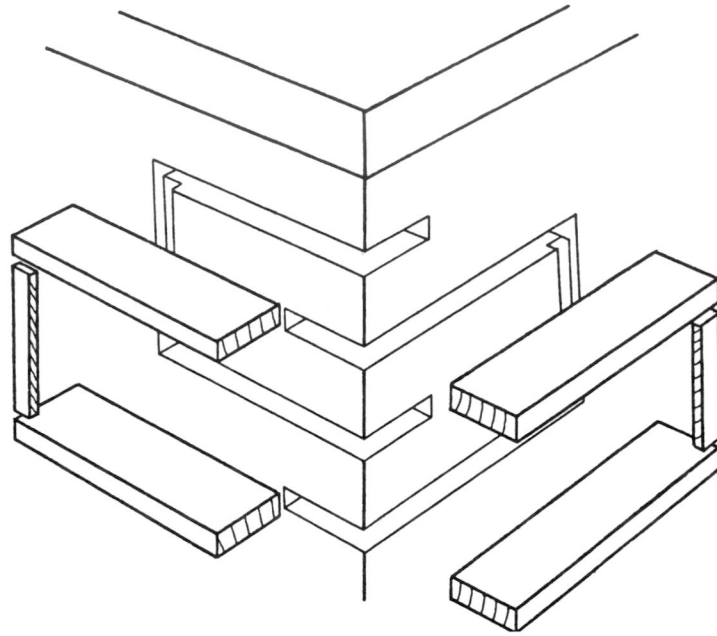

Figure 26 *Mitre and stopped-strip inserts with ends joined by inlays.*

the varying finger width seen in diagram 157 (*see p. 71*) is a good example of this. The number of inserted strips in a finger corresponds to its increase in width, creating a visually complex joint with exceptional strength due to high gluing area (*diagram 168* and *figure 27*).

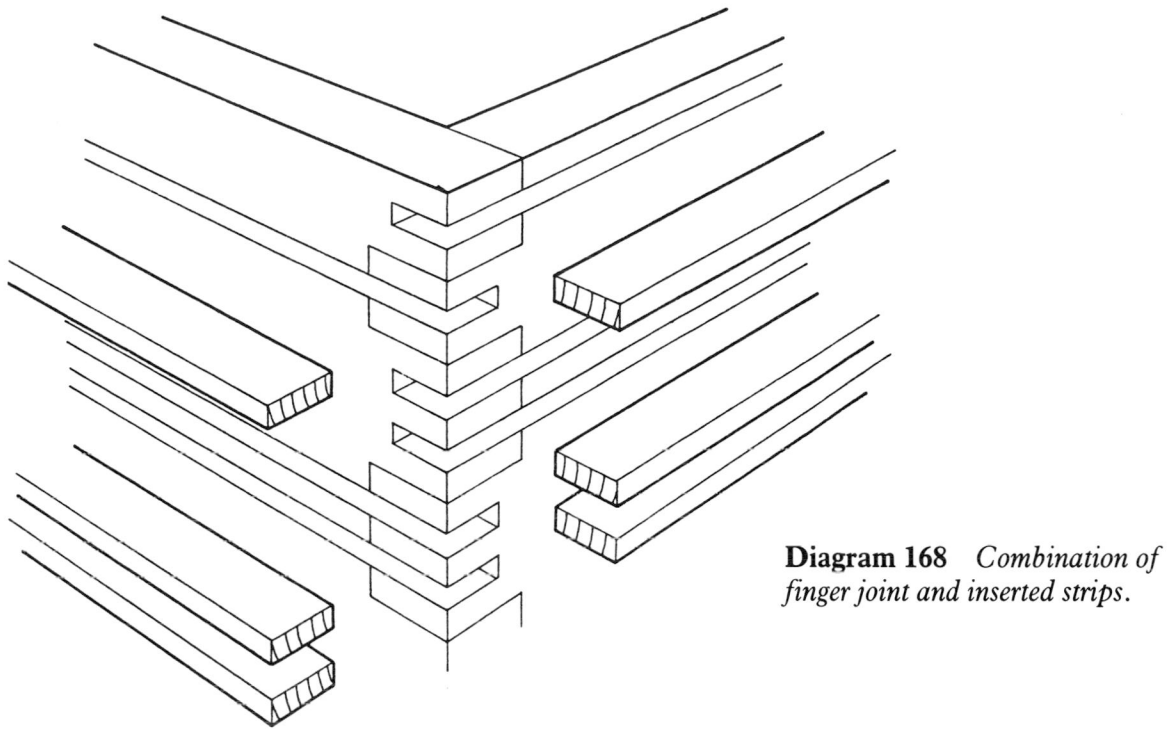

Diagram 168 *Combination of finger joint and inserted strips.*

Figure 27 *Combination of finger joint and strip inserts.*

Mitre joint with dowel

The use of an inserted dowel is another simple yet effective method of introducing decoration to a mitred corner. By introducing it in a diagonal plane along the mitre (*diagram 169*) a very strong joint is produced which provides interest in the elliptical end grain. Drilling the holes must be

Diagram 169   *The dowel runs perpendicular to the mitre line.*

extremely accurate for the dowels to be positioned symmetrically to each other and the corner. To achieve this, a simple jig is made to cramp on the corner which will guide the drill bit accurately (*diagram 170*). In addition to this, some form of support is needed to prevent the timber from splitting as the bit emerges from the carcase. This is most effectively done by gluing a strip of waste timber to the carcase which can be planed away easily after completing the drilling operation.

The dowels are made to be a hand-push fit into the holes; if they are tight and need to be driven in, the glue line of the mitre may break. Prior to gluing the dowels in position, one end should be chamfered to assist location (*diagram 171*).

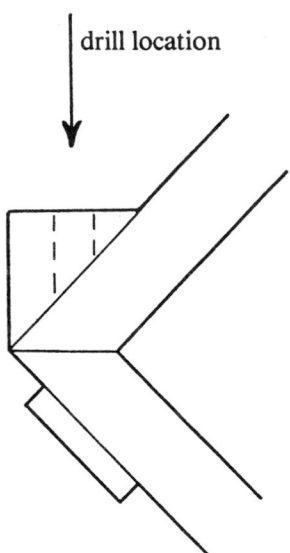

Diagram 170   *A simple jig helps locate the drill bit.*

Diagram 171   *Dowel location is assisted by chamfering one end.*

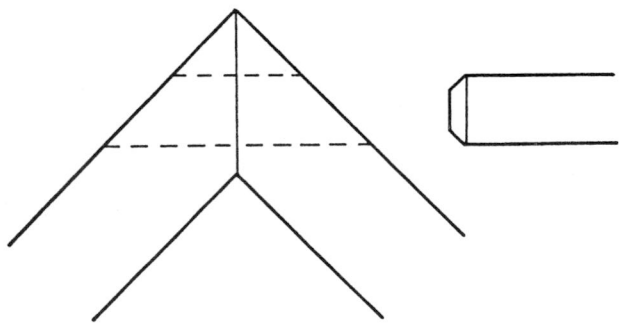

When they have been glued in, the excess is planed away, working into the carcase all the time (*diagram 172*).

By replacing the finger joint with a butt mitre in figure 16 (*see p. 65*), further use of the dowel and mitre combination is found (*diagram 173* and *figure 28*). The placement of the dowels can form any configuration and is really left up to the

direction of planing

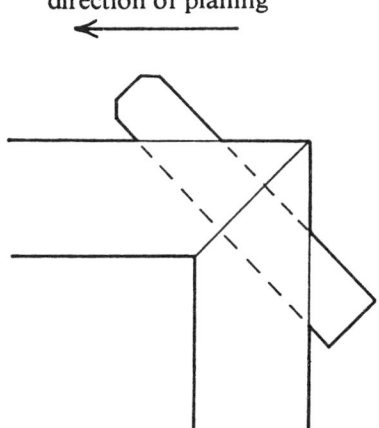

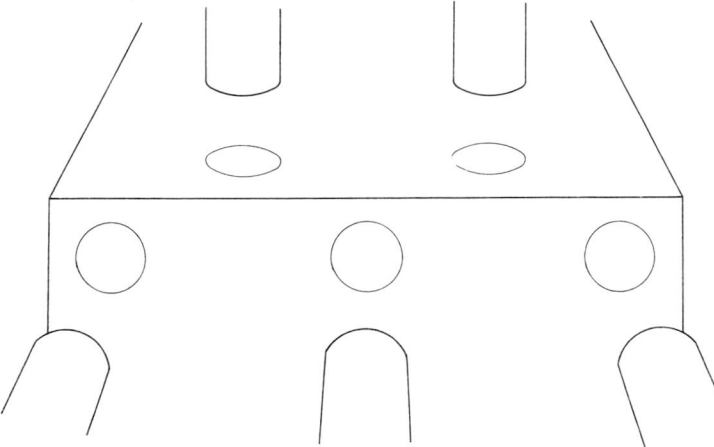

Diagram 172   *Plane into the carcase to remove dowel waste.*

Diagram 173   *Dowel and mitre combination.*

Figure 28   *Mitre with dowel combination.*

81

maker's choice, although they should be used on both surfaces to lock the joint securely. Cutting the holes accurately, preferably with a brad point drill bit, is essential if a neat, symmetrical joint is to be made.

One further variation of mitre/dowel combination that provides for greater interest, uses the same method of construction as diagram 173, but moves the centre of the hole nearer the edge so that part of the dowel protrudes above the surface of the carcase (*diagram 174* and *figure 29*). More than

Diagram 174 *Dowel protrudes through the surface of each panel.*

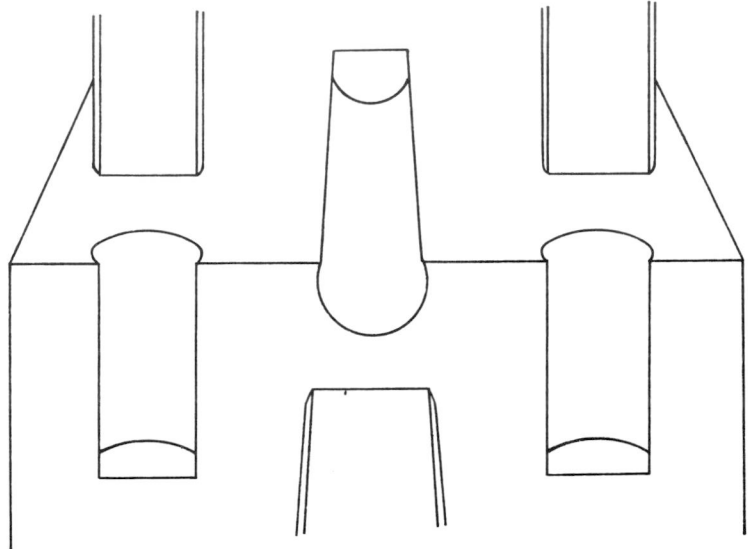

Figure 29 *Mitre with dowel protruding above the surface.*

one half of the dowel should be retained so that it acts as a locking device.

To provide a clean-cut hole on the outside surface, use a forstner bit that will give neat, parallel edges and a flat bottom. When the dowels have been inserted, the exposed part can either be left proud or made flush to the carcase. The dowels can be linked up across the ends by inlaying a strip of timber across the grain to give a further variation (*diagram 175* and *figure 30*).

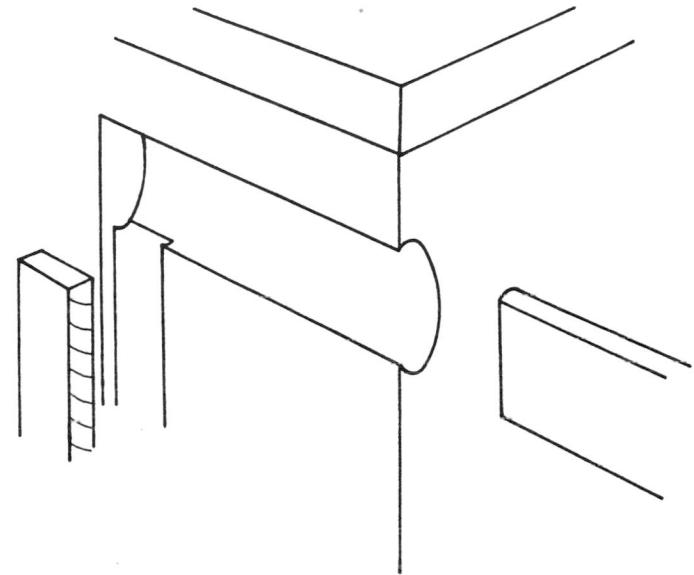

Diagram 175   *The ends of the dowels can be joined by a veneer inlay.*

Figure 30   *Mitre with dowel ends joined by inlays.*

4 Splicing Joints

Before the introduction of adhesives and metal reinforcements, the difficulty in obtaining the long lengths of timber required for some architectural structures led to the development of a splicing or scarf joint that could be used to connect shorter timbers. This became an important feature in both Eastern and Western societies; the great revolution in Japanese joinery being in the Yayoi period (200 B.C.-A.D. 250), while in England it lasted from the twelfth to the sixteenth century. It was a style of jointing that hadn't been seen before and was left entirely to the woodworker's imagination. Increasingly intricate forms were created in an attempt to achieve the maximum strength. Many woodworkers will find the intricacies of splicing quite fascinating and, although their use is not essential because of modern adhesives, will no doubt want to experience the complexities of cutting such joinery.

ENGLISH SCARF JOINTS
Splayed scarf joints

At the start of the twelfth century in England, the predominating scarf joint was the splayed type with some variations being the strongest examples of spliced joints ever produced. The stop-splayed scarf, using the under-squinted and sallied butt with four face pegs and one face key which is twice edge-pegged (*diagram 176*), is a good example of the concept behind this type of construction.

Both halves of the joint are identical, therefore marking out can be done at the same time for each component. Since the angle of splay will depend on the length and width of joint, all examples in this section will be discussed with a length of two-and-a-half times the width of timber. Sections of timber will be 4cm (1½in.) square with a joint length of 10cm (3¾in.), any variation in size always being to this proportion.

84

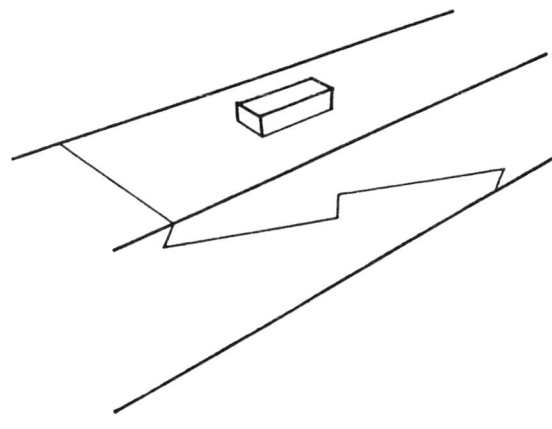

Diagram 176 *Stop-splayed scarf, using under-squinted and sallied butt, with four face pegs and one face key which is twice edge-pegged.*

The extremities of the joint are set in by 5mm (³⁄₁₆in.) from the upper and lower surface, and the two points connected to give the angle of splay. The butted ends are then taken to the outside at an angle of 60° (*diagram 177*). The outline of the joint is completed by squaring across from the outer edge. All lines should be made with a knife and sliding bevel.

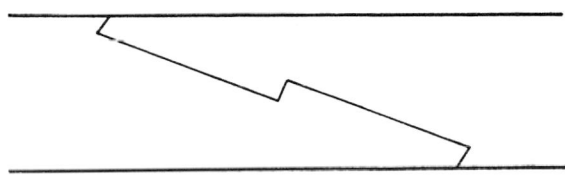

Diagram 177 *Outline of the joint on the edge of the timber.*

Sawcuts are made as close to the lines as possible, which should remove most of the waste, the remainder being cut away with a chisel or shoulder plane (*diagram 178*). The

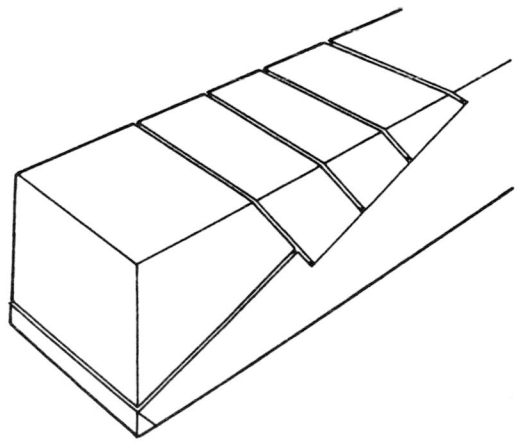

Diagram 178 *Sawcuts are made to assist waste removal.*

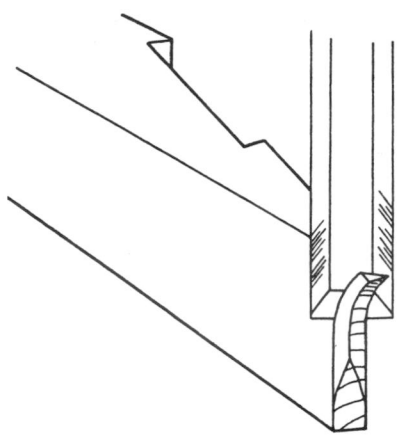

under-squinted square butt is formed by carefully trimming with the paring chisel (*diagram 179*).

To mark out the mortise for the key, the joint should be temporarily pushed together. A section of 2 x 1cm (¾ x ⅜in.) is drawn in a symmetrical position on the top surface and taken round the sides to the bottom at an angle of 15° (*diagram 180*). The lines on the side can be off-set by 1mm

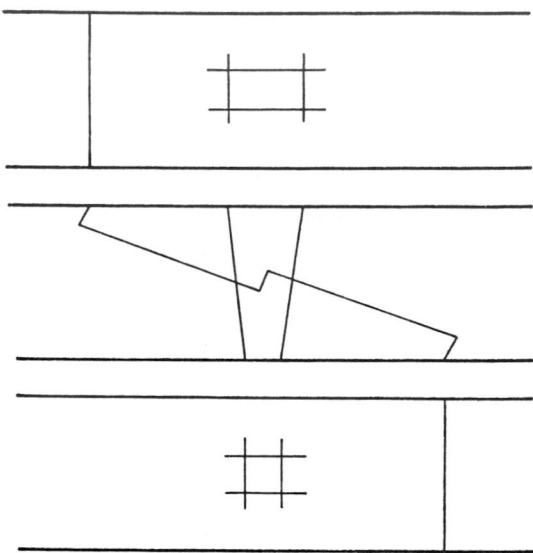

Diagram 179   *The under-squinted square butt is trimmed with a paring chisel.*

Diagram 180   *Marking out the mortise to accept the face key.*

(¹⁄₃₂in.) so that a compressive force is created when the key is driven into the mortise (*diagram 181*). When the joint is

Diagram 181   *Off-set mortise helps create a compressive force when the key is driven in.*

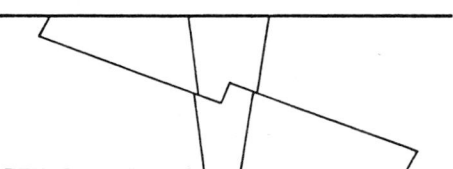

taken apart, the lines on each side are squared across the splay and the width of the mortise marked in with the mortise gauge (*diagram 182*).

To cut the mortise, remove most of the waste with the brace and bit, and trim back to the lines using the mortise and paring chisels. A key is then shaped to correspond to the angle of the mortise and driven in when the joint is together

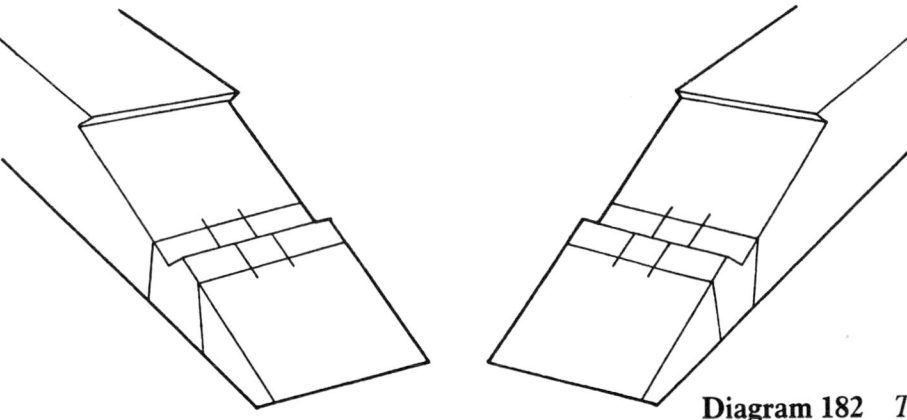

(diagram 183). The pegs that secure the key are set in a central position on each half of the joint with a diameter of 4mm (⁵⁄₃₂in.). The pegs on the top surface, also with a 4mm (⁵⁄₃₂in.) diameter, are set in by 1cm (²⁄₅in.) from the edge and 2cm (⁴⁄₅in.) from the end *(diagram 184)*. They should be square to the upper surface.

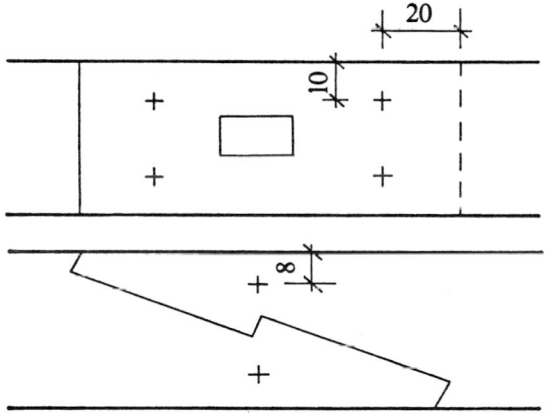

Diagram 182 *The outline of the mortise should be scribed across each splay.*

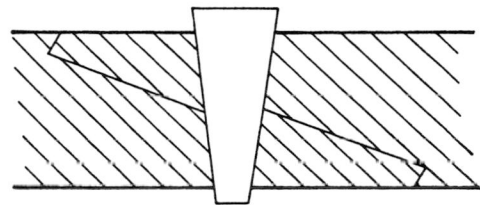

Diagram 183 *Section through the joint showing the face key in position.*

Diagram 184 *Location of face pegs.*

A development from this last example into what is probably the strongest type of splayed scarf joint uses under-squinted square butts with transverse key and four face pegs *(diagram 185* and *figure 31)*. Its basic principles can be found in Roman ship construction, English and Japanese architecture and Chinese furniture. The insertion of the key forces the joint together, closing the butts and creating compression at the splay, giving great mechanical efficiency. The addition of four dowels perpendicular to the splay prevents any lateral movement.

Diagram 185 *Splayed scarf using under-squinted butts with transverse key and four face pegs.*

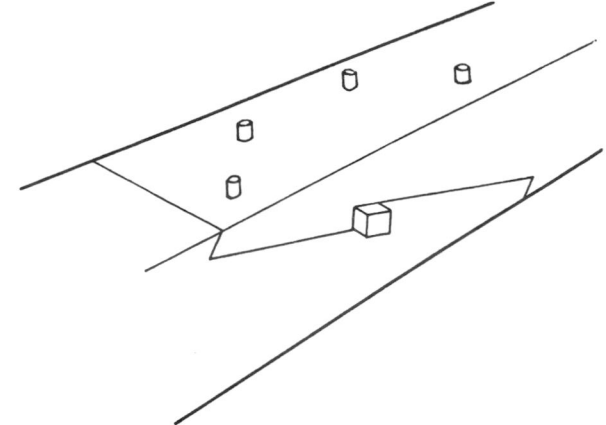

Figure 31 *Splayed scarf with under-squinted square butts, transverse key and four face pegs.*

Again, the two halves of the joint are identical and can be marked together. The end of the square butt is set in by 5mm (³⁄₁₆in.) and then taken back to the outside at an angle of 60°. Parallel lines should then be drawn in, connecting the inner point to the opposite outer edge (*diagram 186*). At the centre

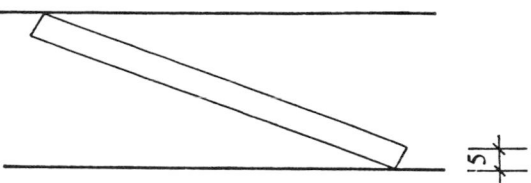

Diagram 186 *Profile of the joint on the timber's edge.*

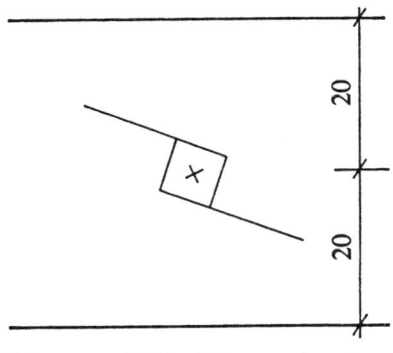

Diagram 187 *The termination of each splay forms the mortise to accept the transverse key.*

of these lines, a square should be marked in to signify the mortise for the key and the termination of the tabled splay (*diagram 187*).

The removal of the waste is similar to cutting parts of a bridle joint. Having squared round all marking-out lines, saw cuts are made, terminating at the lower splay (*diagram 188*) with extra cuts made in between to assist timber removal. The waste should be pared away, initially taking off the corners from both sides and gradually working to a flat plane (*diagram 189*). The upper splay of the joint can then be

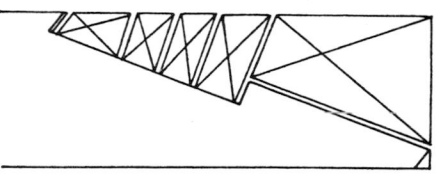

Diagram 188 *Sawcuts assist waste removal.*

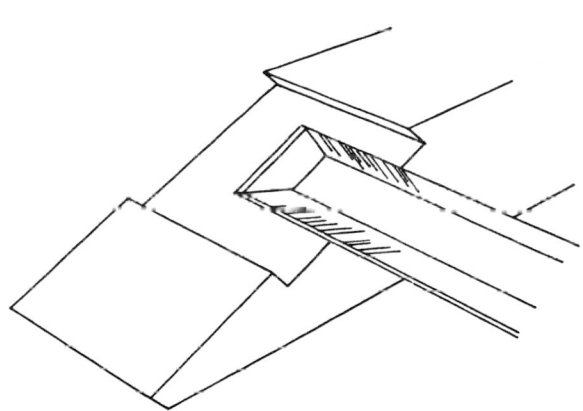

Diagram 189 *The splay is flattened with a paring chisel.*

finished, first removing most of the waste with the saw and then planing back to the line to give a flat surface. The under-squinting is then trimmed back and the square ends planed to the corresponding angle of 60°. The joint should now go together.

Prepare a key to fit into the mortise so that the joint tightens when it is driven in. Holes of 4mm (5/32in.) diameter can then be drilled perpendicular to the splay and the dowels inserted. Connect the diagonals of each splay and set in the centre of the holes by 1.5cm (⅝in.) from the corner (*diagram 190*).

Diagram 190   *Location of dowel centres on the splay.*

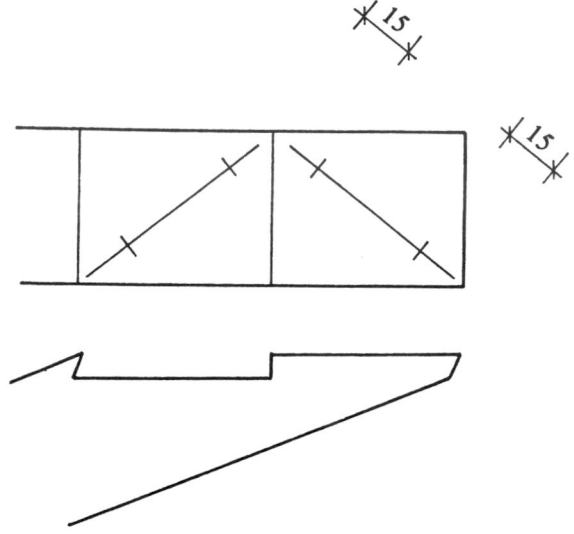

Edge-halved scarf

The inevitable development in this style of jointing saw a transition from the splayed type to the edge-halving with the stop-splayed scarf. This has vertical bridled butts and incorporates four face pegs and two edge pegs (*diagram 191* and *figure 32*) combining both elements.

Figure 32   *Stop-splayed scarf with vertical bridled butts, four face pegs and two edge pegs.*

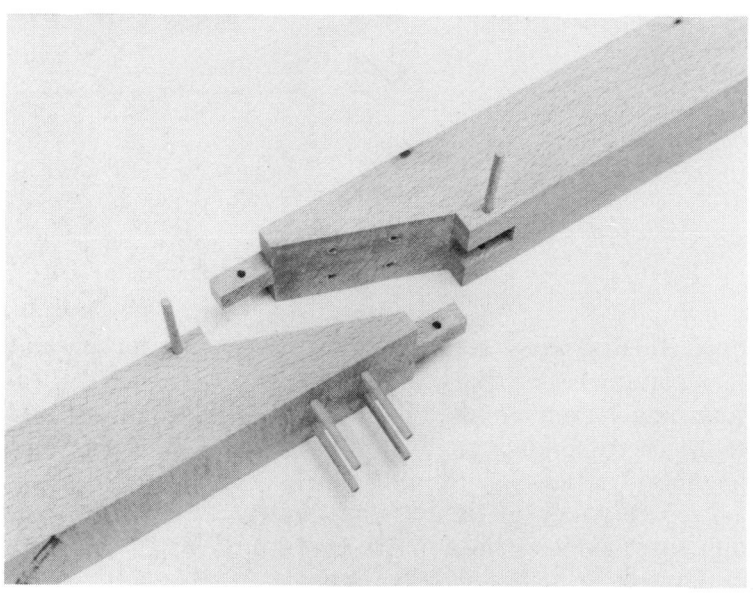

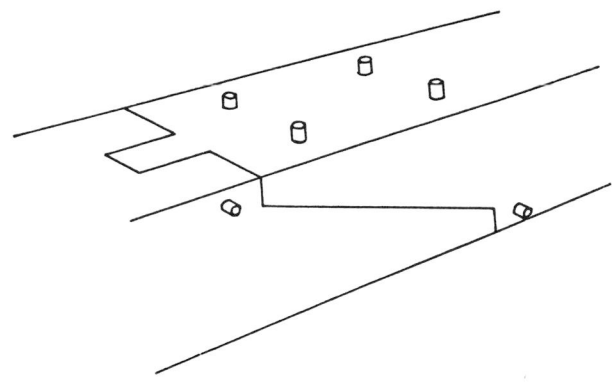

The length and depth of the bridled end is 2cm (¾in.) and 8mm (⁵⁄₁₆in.) respectively and should be marked on the side of each piece of timber. The angle of splay is ascertained by connecting the two internal corners. The width of the bridle is 1cm (³⁄₈in.) and should be marked symmetrically on both top and bottom surfaces (*diagram 192*).

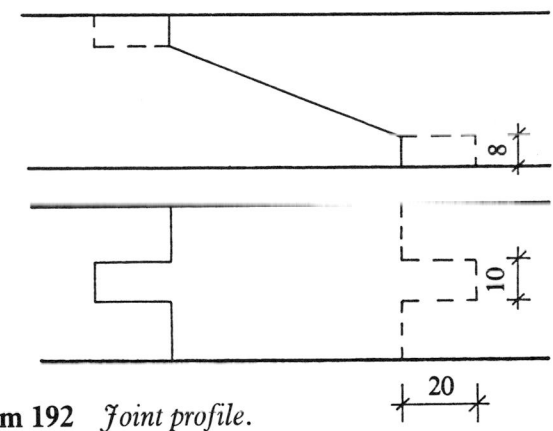

Diagram 192 *Joint profile.*

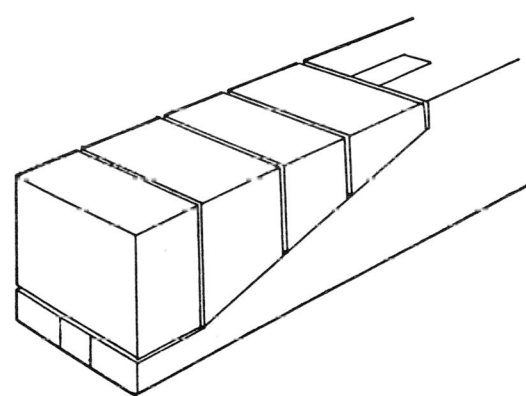

Diagram 193 *Sawcuts assist waste removal.*

Sawcuts should be made to remove most of the waste around the bridle and at intermediate points along the length to assist removal of waste from the splay (*diagram 193*). All waste should then be removed, trimming back to the lines with the aid of a paring chisel and shoulder plane (*diagram 194*). To remove the waste of the mortise, make diagonal sawcuts connecting the two inner points (*diagram 195*). Timber can then be chopped out with a suitable sized mortise chisel, with any necessary trimming of the sides done with

Diagram 194 *Either a paring chisel or a shoulder plane can be used to trim the splay.*

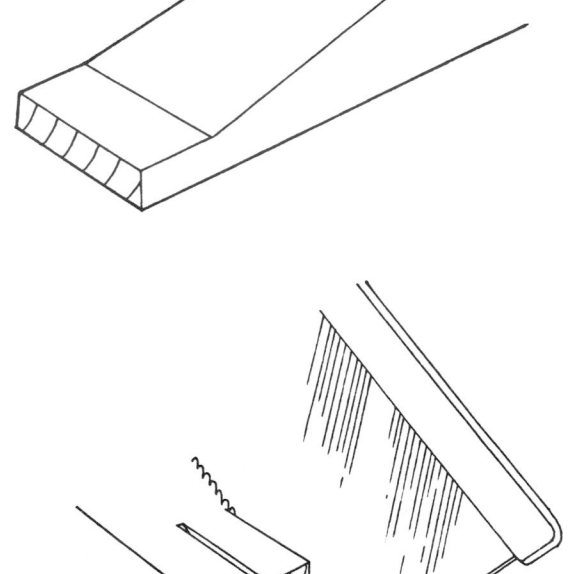

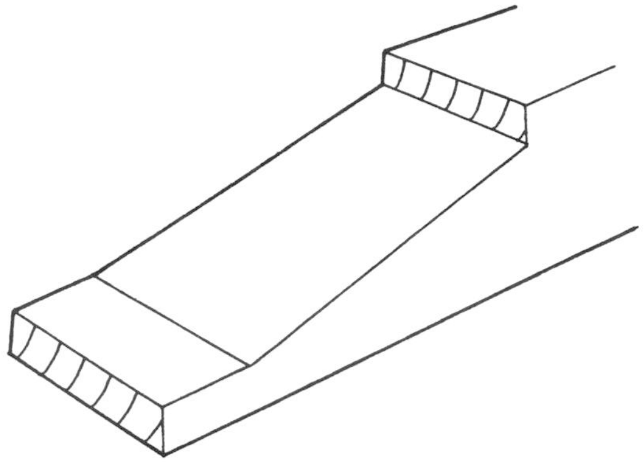

Diagram 195 *Diagonal sawcuts help to remove mortise waste.*

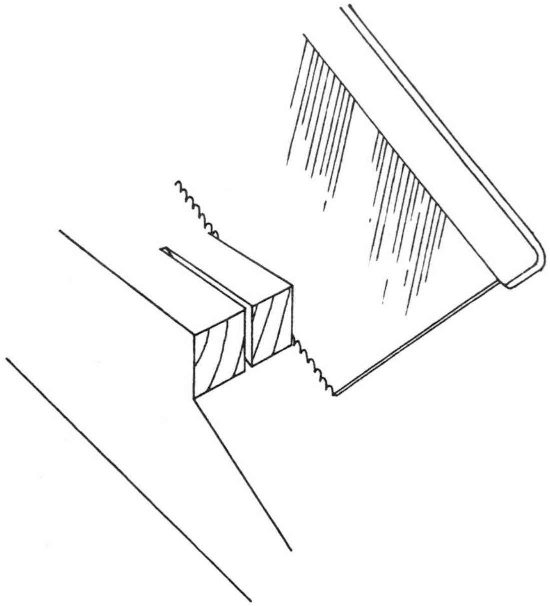

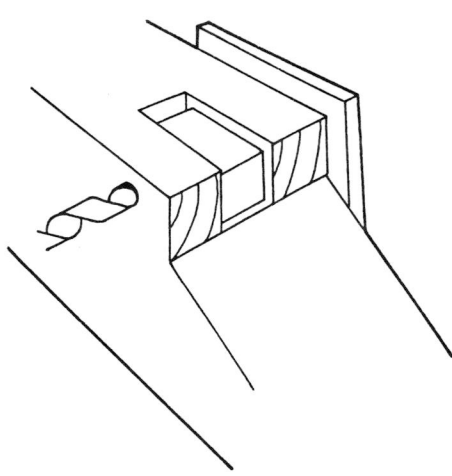

Diagram 196 *Waste prevents timber breakout when drilling the hole for the edge peg.*

the paring chisel. Care should be taken to ensure that the mortise is flat-bottomed.

A symmetrically positioned hole of 3mm (⅛in.) diameter is drilled from the side through the mortise, with waste timber being used to prevent breakout as the bit emerges (*diagram 196*). The joint can then be pushed together and the centre for the hole in the tenon found by using that through the mortise as a guide. The centre can be slightly offset, which will help draw the joint together when the dowel is driven in.

When the joint is together, the four holes on the face can be drilled to accept dowels of 3mm (⅛in.) diameter. These should be set in by 1cm (³⁄₈in.) from the edge and 2cm (³⁄₄in.) from the termination of the splay (*diagram 197*).

A similar type of joint shows the full use of the edge-halved scarf at the expense of the splay and is cut in a similar manner (*diagram 198*).

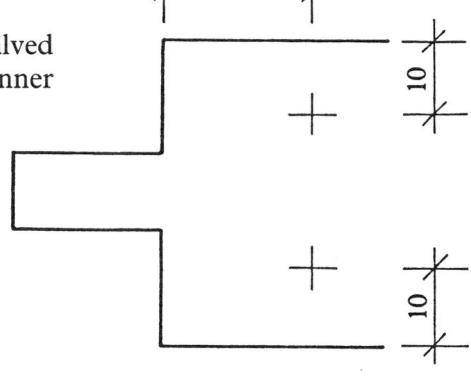

Diagram 197   *Location of face pegs.*

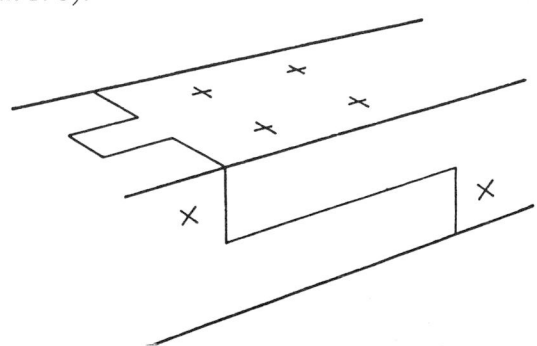

Diagram 198   *Full edge-halved scarf similar to diagram 191.*

Face-halved and bladed scarf

The third significant style of scarf joint developed in the British Isles was the bladed type, the face-halved and bladed scarf with thick central peg and four edge pegs being a typical example (*diagram 199*).

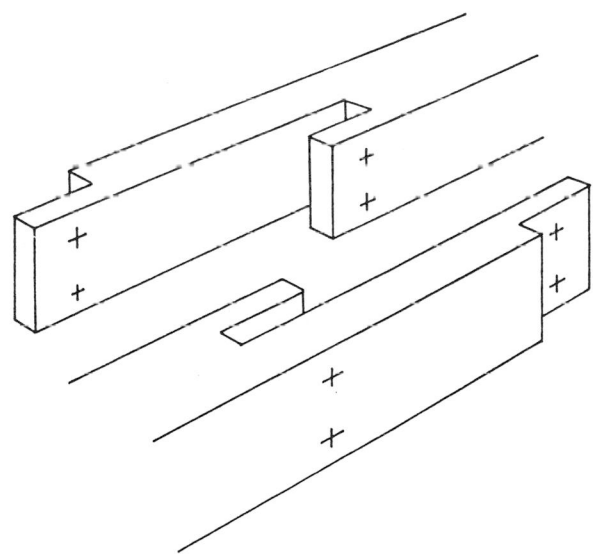

Diagram 199   *Face-halved and bladed scarf with thick central peg and four face pegs.*

A mortise gauge is set to approximately 1cm (³⁄₈in.) between points (to the nearest mortise chisel), and from point to fence so that when working from both edges the outer point scribes the same line (*diagram 200*). The

Diagram 200   *Profile of joint on each component.*

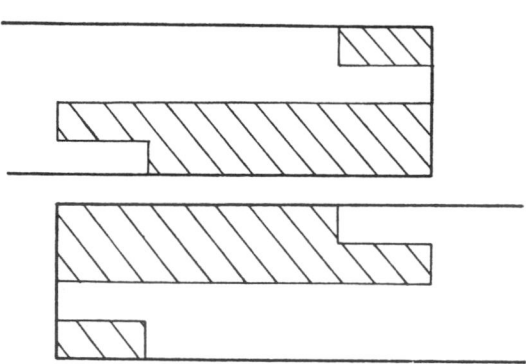

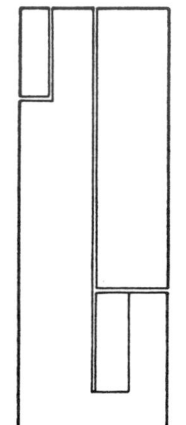

Diagram 201   *Sawcuts are made to remove most of the waste.*

Diagram 202   *The final cut is made on the inside face of the mortise.*

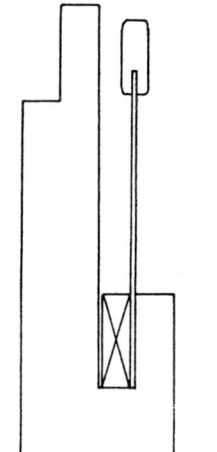

Diagram 203   *Dowel location on the edge of the joint.*

shoulders of the two outer quarters should be set in by 2.5cm (1in.) from the end.

The outer part of the tenon is formed by making two simple sawcuts close to the marked lines which will remove most of the waste, with any necessary trimming done with the paring chisel and shoulder plane. A long saw cut has to be made on the waste side of the centre line which may be too long for a standard tenon saw, in which case a panel saw or preferably a Japanese Ryoba saw should be used (*diagram 201*). A sawcut across the end of the outside tenon will remove more of the waste, which leaves one final cut to be made on the inside face of the mortise (*diagram 202*). The final piece of waste is removed with a coping saw and any necessary trimming done on all surfaces.

The process of drilling the holes should be repeated, as in the previous example, so that the joint is tightened when the dowels (3mm diameter, [⅛in.]) are driven in. Their centres are located 1.25cm (½in.) from the end of the tenon and 1cm (⅜in.) from the upper and lower face (*diagram 203*). The

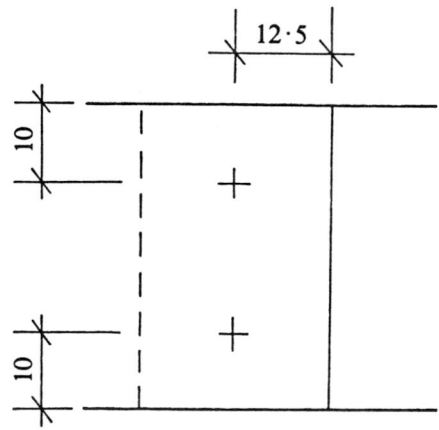

94

joint is then put together, a central hole of 5mm (³/₁₆in.) diameter drilled and a matching dowel fitted.

By the eighteenth century, the introduction of iron plates and bolts as strengtheners virtually ended the use of the purely wooden scarf joint.

Edge-halved scarf with under-squinted butts

One other significant example of a scarf joint used in Western societies was designed by the Greene brothers and used on the interiors of their buildings, particularly in the Gamble house. As the brothers were strongly influenced by the Japanese style, obvious links can be seen in the construction, the edge-halved scarf with under-squinted butts with securing peg (*diagram 204*) being typical. To emphasize the joint, all corners were slightly rounded.

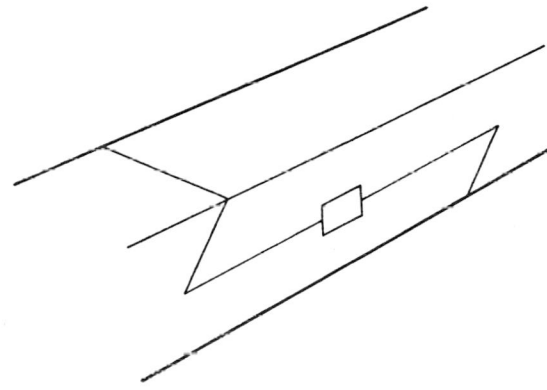

Diagram 204   *Edge-halved scarf with under-squinted butts and securing peg.*

Using a marking gauge set at 2cm (³/₄in.) scribe in the halving on both edges of each component. The angle of the under-squint is taken from the centre to the outside at an angle of 60° using a sliding bevel and knife (*diagram 205*).

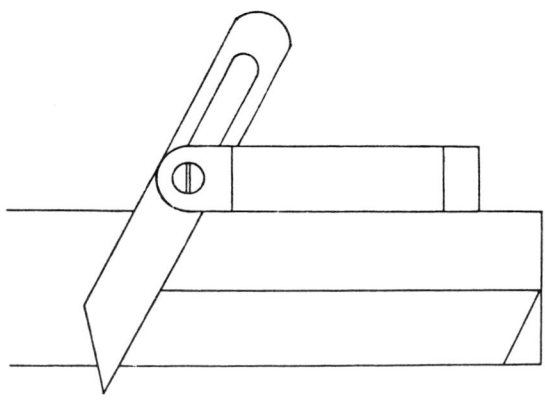

Diagram 205   *The angle of the under-squint is marked with a knife and sliding bevel.*

The lines are then squared across the top and bottom face to complete the outline of the joint.

The majority of waste can be removed with the tenon saw, making cuts on the waste side of the lines. The halving and under-squinted shoulder can be trimmed back with the paring chisel and shoulder plane if necessary, with the end being planed to the correct angle (*diagram 206*).

Diagram 206 *Profile of the scarf cut on the end of one component.*

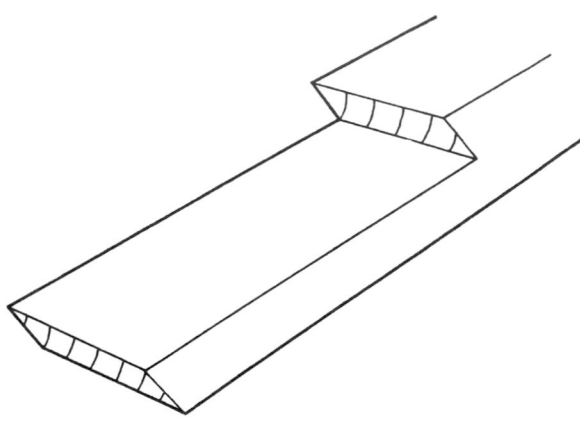

The next step is to cut a housing on each halving, which will create a mortise to accept the key when the joint is put together. This should be set in from the end by 4cm with a dimension of 2cm x 5mm (¾ x ³⁄₁₆in.) (*diagram 207*). If the

Diagram 207 *Positioning of mortise.*

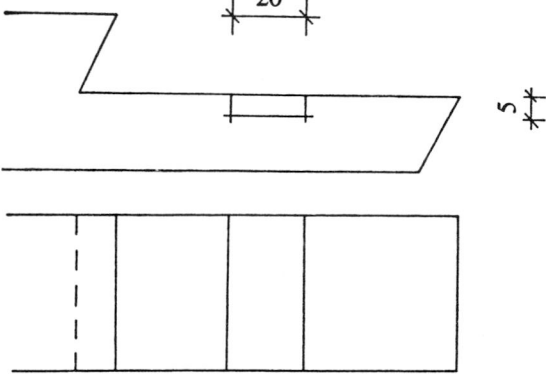

Diagram 208 *Off-set mortise will create a compressive force when the peg is driven in.*

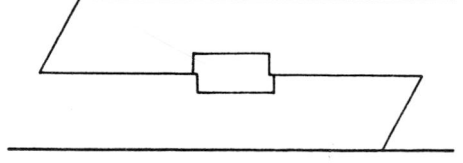

two halvings are slightly off-set when put together, the joint will be tightened as the key is driven in (*diagram 208*). When making the key, ensure that pressure is not exerted at the bottom of each housing as this will tend to push the joint apart.

96

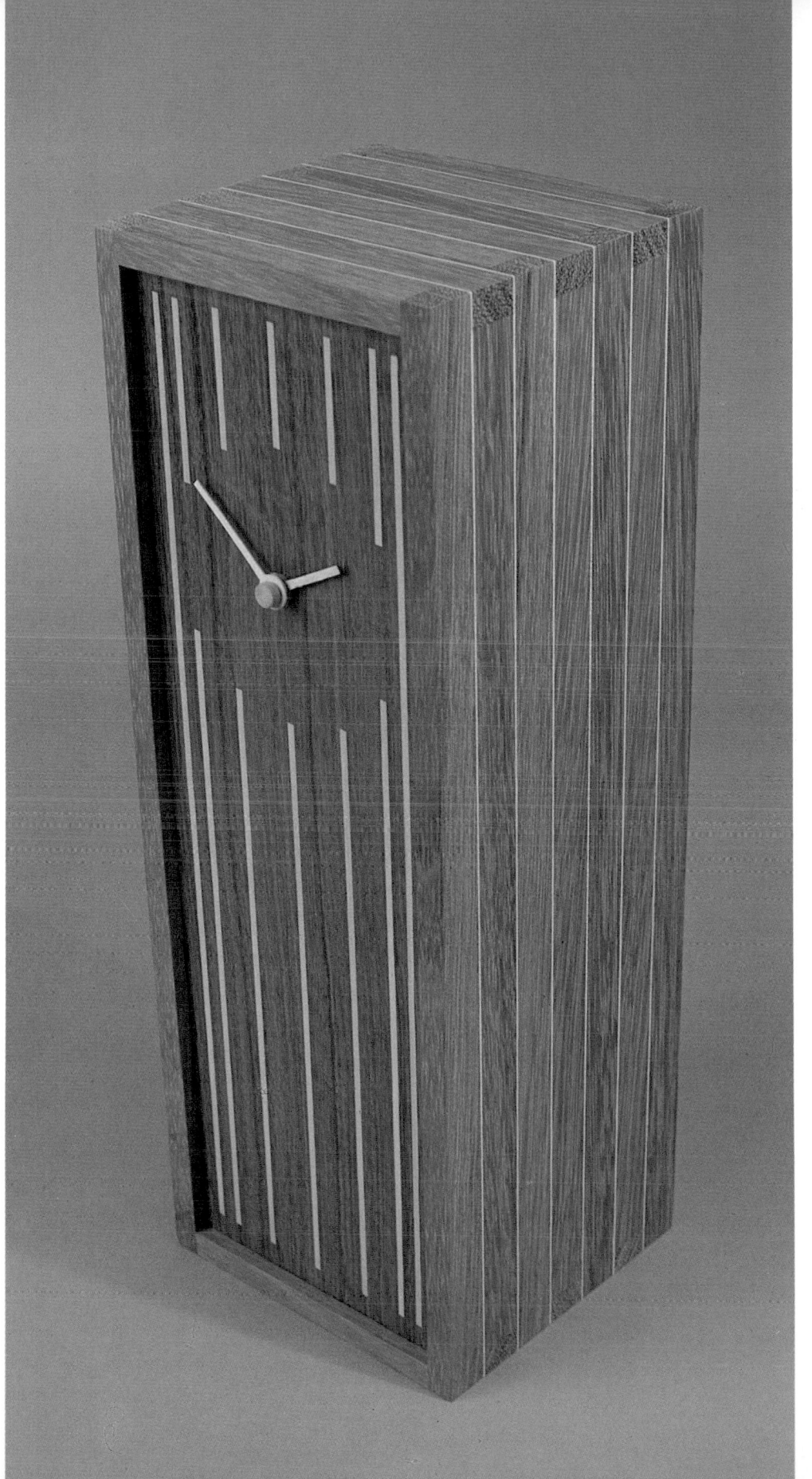

5 Mantel clock in
black bean and
sycamore

6 Chest of drawers in black bean and English oak

7 Dining table in wenge and Japanese oak

EASTERN SCARF JOINTS

Japanese architecture has undoubtedly been one of the most influential styles of wooden construction. With the introduction of iron tools in the Yayoi period (200 B.C.-A.D. 250), their style advanced to the post and lintel system which allowed a greater architectural freedom. Differences obviously occur in their approach which had considerable effect on style, the most significant being the use of the saw and plane. They cut on the pull rather than the push which gives them a greater accuracy but a loss of cutting power.

Kanawa-tsugi (mortised, rebated, oblique scarf)

The Japanese style of construction, a simple post-beam framework without any braces or struts, required the use of strong, accurately executed joinery. The splicing joint has many different configurations with the more complex being particularly interesting. *Kanawa-tsugi* (mortised, rebated, oblique scarf joint; *diagram 209* and *figure 33*) is, without

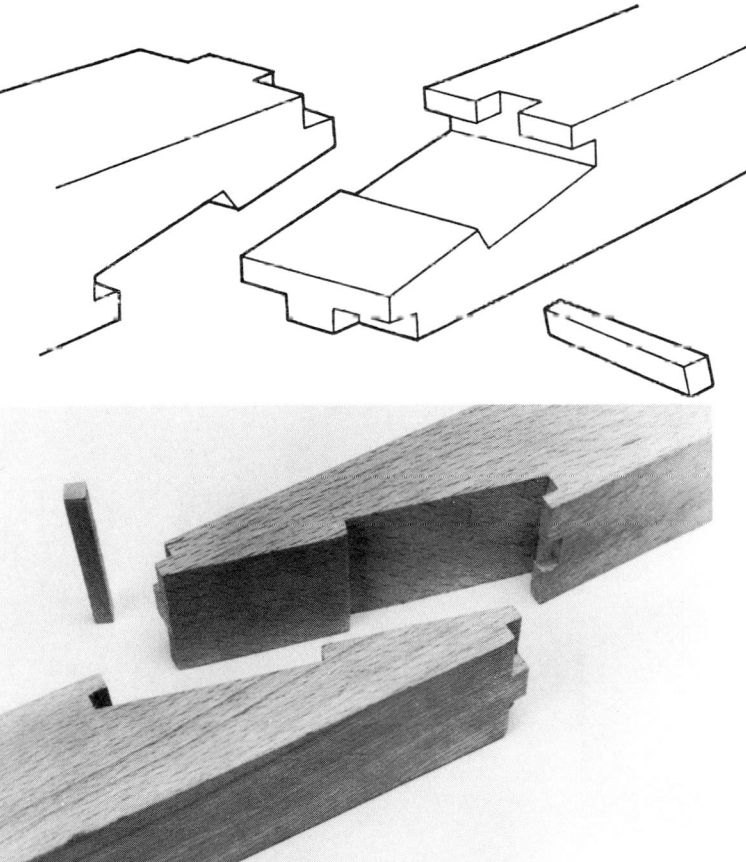

Diagram 209   Kanawa-tsugi *(mortised, rebated, oblique scarf joint)*.

Figure 33   Kanawa-tsugi *(mortised, rebated, oblique scarf joint)*.

doubt, the most fascinating, and probably the strongest type of dry joint produced by the Japanese. The stub tenons cut into the mortised ends prevent any lateral movement, but an adjustment to the internal faces is necessary to get the joint together in this way. This is achieved by reducing their total length by that of the stub tenons, taking an equal amount off each face. The key to fit in the resulting mortise forces the joint together in a similar way to the strong English type (*see diagram 185*). The stub tenon makes it slightly stronger than the under-squinted version.

Using 4cm (1½in.) square, sectioned timber with a 10cm (3¾in.) long splice, the joint is marked out as illustrated (*diagram 210*). The angle of the splay is found by connecting

Diagram 210   *Profile of the splicing joint.*

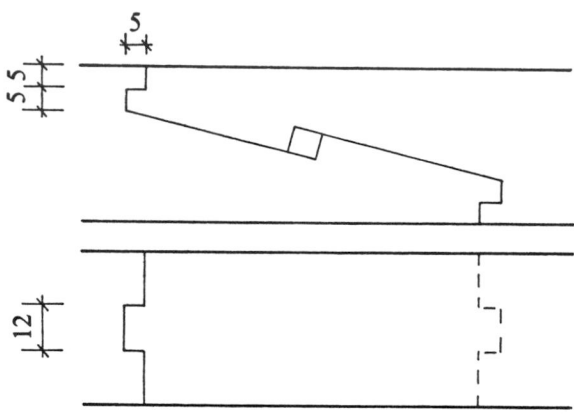

the two points of the inner mortise with the corners of the stub tenon, with the key being located centrally between the two lines. The stub mortise and tenon should be marked centrally at a width of 1cm on the top and bottom face.

The stub tenons should be formed initially so that the waste timber of the splay can be used as a support (*diagram 212*). Two simple sawcuts will remove the main bulk of waste

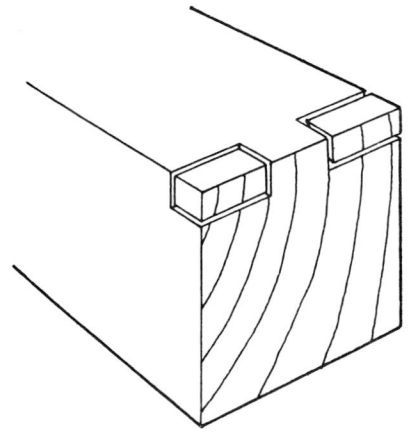

Diagram 211   *The diagonal sawcuts help form the stub tenons.*

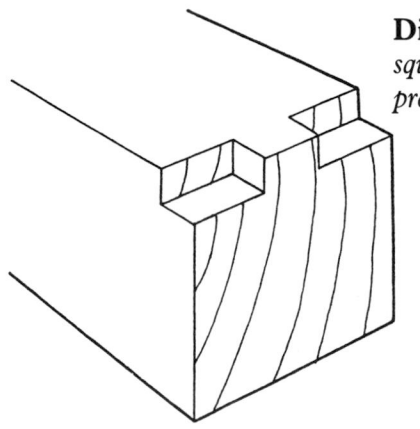

Diagram 212   *A clean, square corner should be produced.*

at the splay, with the upper half being planed flat (*diagram 213*). The lower level of the two-tiered splay is created by paring away the waste in the same way as a halving is cut (*diagram 214*). The next step is to cut the mortise that accepts

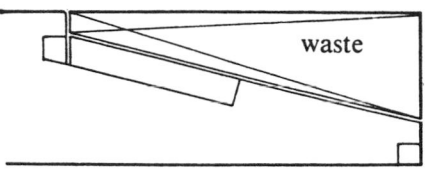

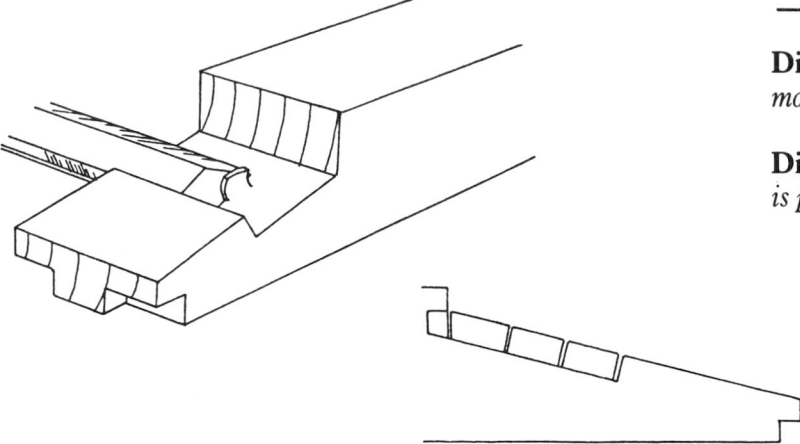

Diagram 213 *Sawcuts remove most of the waste.*

Diagram 214 *The lower splay is pared away.*

the stub tenon, initially chopping down from the top face so that timber breakout is prevented by the remaining waste (*diagram 215*).

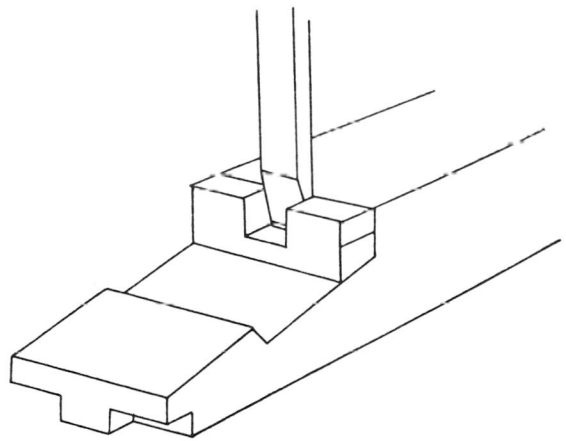

Diagram 215 *Cutting the mortise that accepts the stub tenon.*

When all corners have been thoroughly cleaned out, the joint should go together. A key is then made to fit the mortise which is driven in to secure the joint.

Having developed such a strong joint in comparison to earlier examples, it was inevitable that variations would be used. *Okkake-daisen-tsugi* (rebated oblique scarf joint) is a similar joint, but lacks the securing key, which is replaced by

Diagram 216 Okkake-daisen-tsugi (*rebated, oblique scarf joint*).

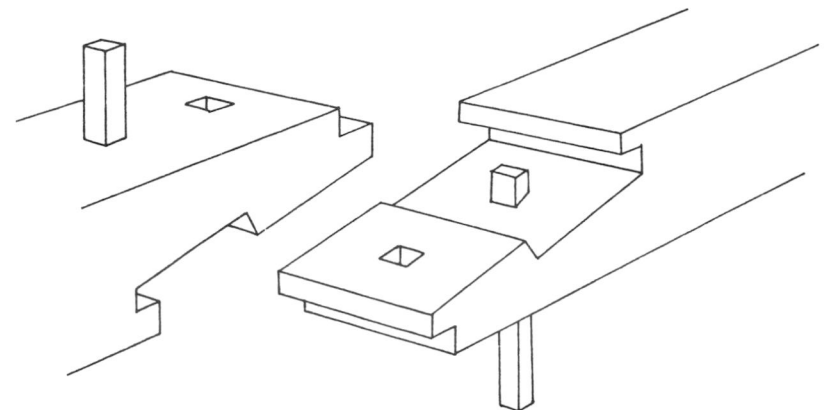

a pair of pegs running through the splay (*diagram 216*). The joint can be tightened by off-setting the mortise on each component to draw it together as the pegs are driven in (*diagram 217*).

Diagram 217 *Off-set mortises will draw the joint together.*

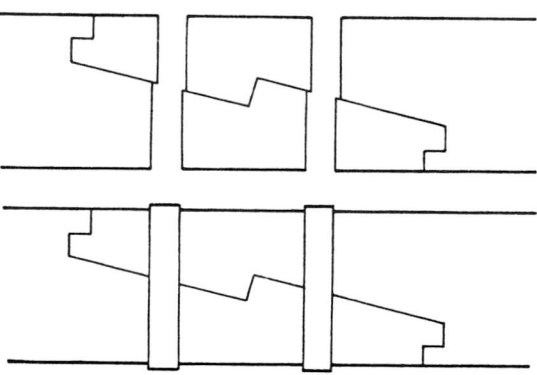

Chinese scarf joint

A similar joint to the *Kanawa-tsugi* was used in the construction of the traditional style of Chinese chair back (*diagram 218*). It was the craftsman's practice to create the curve by using three or, most commonly, five pieces of timber joined end to end in this way, with final finishing done by hand. The process of cutting the joint is the same as *Kanawa-tsugi*, but an additional difficulty is experienced because of the curved sides. Accuracy must be maintained on the inner surfaces as they may be exposed when the final shaping is complete. Further variations were used, but

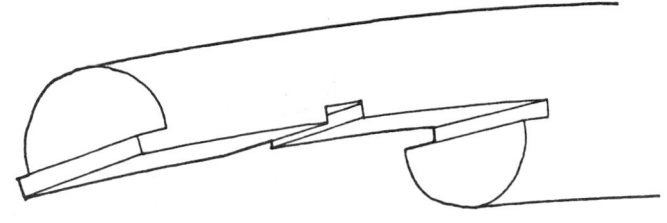

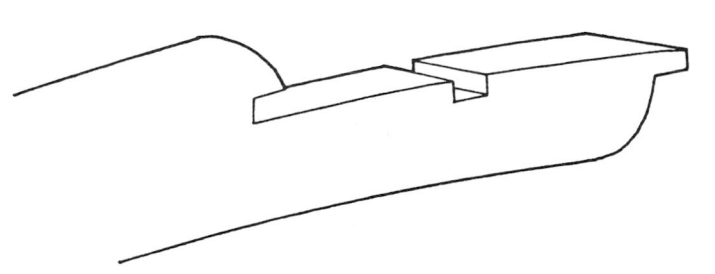

Diagram 218 *Chinese joint used on the traditional chair back.*

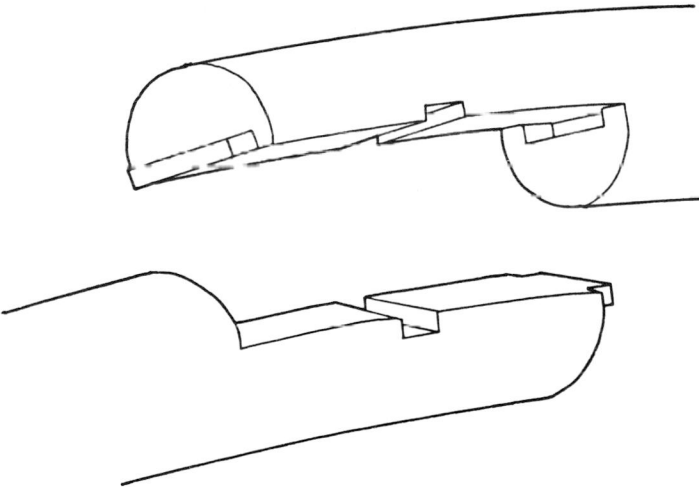

Diagram 219 *Variation of Chinese splicing joint.*

remained the personal choice of individual craftsmen (*diagram 219*).

SPECIALIZED SCARF JOINTS

Many scarf joints were designed for specific situations, such as the *Sao-tsugi* (lapped rod mortise and tenon), used when it was only possible to drop the male member on to the female member (*diagram 220, figure 34*). Many variations on the neck length can be used, but the joint's strength does not increase significantly by making it longer, although, at first sight, this may seem to be the case.

Diagram 220 Sao-tsugi
(*lapped rod mortise and tenon*).

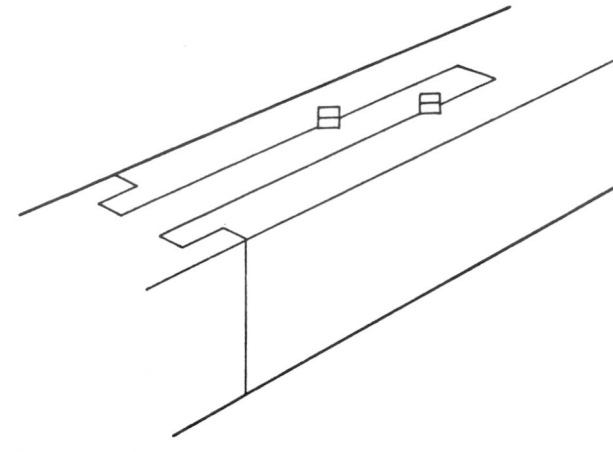

Figure 34 Sao-tsugi (*lapped rod mortise and tenon joint*).

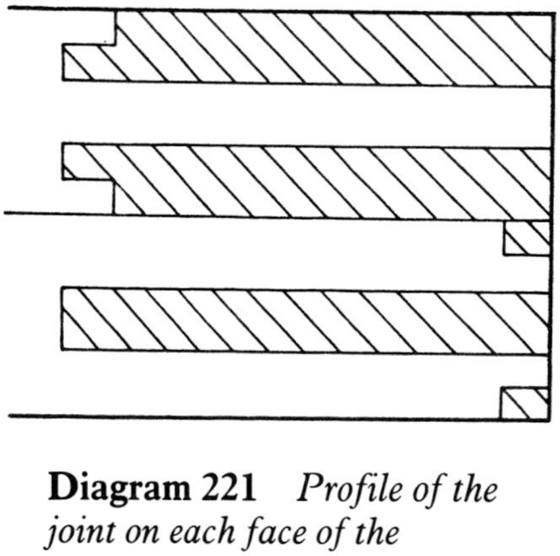

Diagram 221 *Profile of the joint on each face of the components.*

Marking out on the top surface should be done with both pieces of timber fastened together (*diagram 221*). The stub tenon is 1cm x 7mm (⅜ x ¼in.) with the rod tenon scribed centrally at a width of 1.2cm (½in.). The depth of the rod tenon is set in from the top face by 2cm (¾in.). The male component is made first, most of the waste being removed by four sawcuts (*diagram 222*). The mortise that accepts the stub

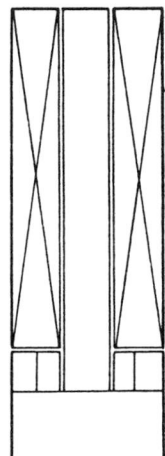

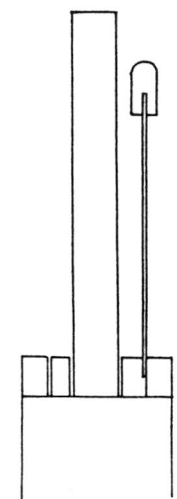

Diagram 222 *Waste removal by sawcuts.*

tenon is then cut using a chisel of appropriate width (*diagram 223*). To complete this part of the joint, the rod tenon has to be reduced in width by 2cm (¾in.), leaving a haunch of 5 mm (³⁄₁₆in.) at the shoulder (*diagram 224*).

Diagram 223 *Removal of waste left in the mortise.*

Diagram 224 *The underface of the joint shows the rod tenon reduced by one-half leaving a haunch of 5mm (¹⁄₁₆in.).*

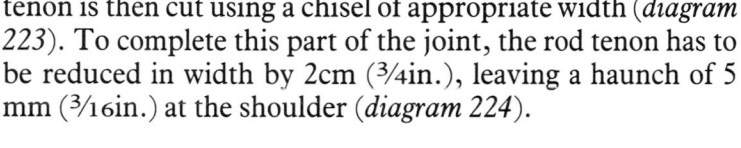

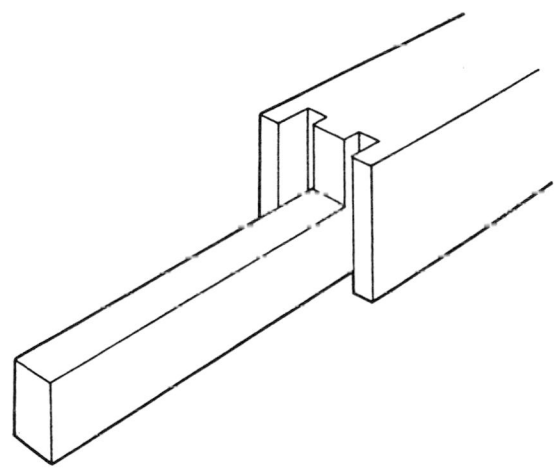

The female component requires a long stopped mortise to be cut, and is made initially by removing the bulk of the waste with a flat-bottomed drill bit and then trimming back to the lines with a mortise chisel of appropriate size. The outer corners of the shoulder should be removed to create the stub tenons, and a mortise cut to accept the haunch of the male member.

With all corners thoroughly cleaned out, the joint can be pushed together and the position of the two keys located.

Diagram 225 *Off-set mortises will help draw the joint together.*

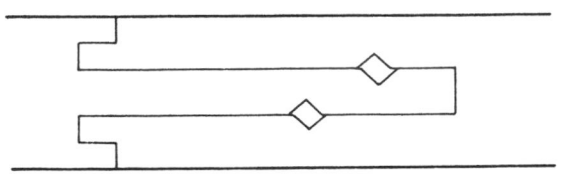

These should be set in from the end by 2cm (¾in.) and 4cm (1½in.) respectively, and set at an angle of 45° to the edge. By slightly off-setting the position of each half of the key, the joint can be pulled together when constructed (*diagram 225*).

Other examples of English (*diagrams 226-228*) and Japanese (*diagrams 229-231*) splicing joints illustrate further variations developed to create a sound construction when used in a particular situation.

Diagram 226 *Stop-splayed scarf with under-squinted and sallied butt, four face pegs and one face key.*

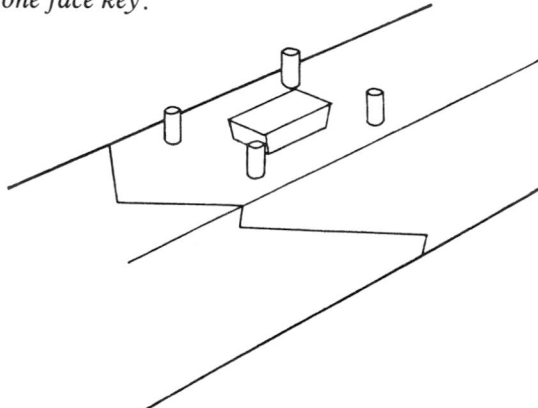

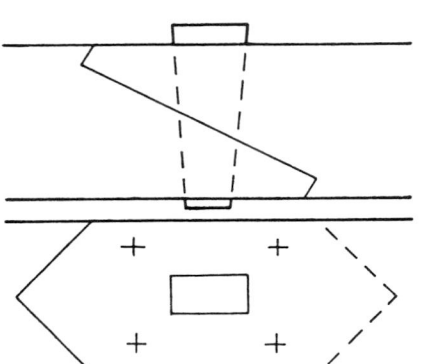

Diagram 227 *Fished scarf with face-housed fish piece and four edge pegs.*

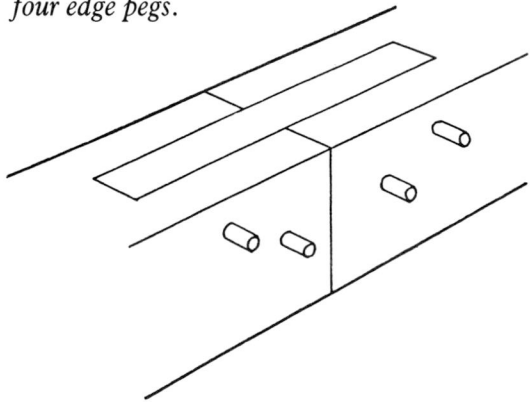

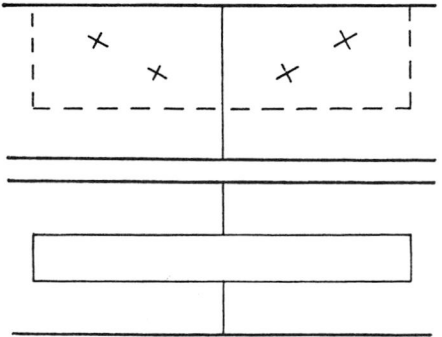

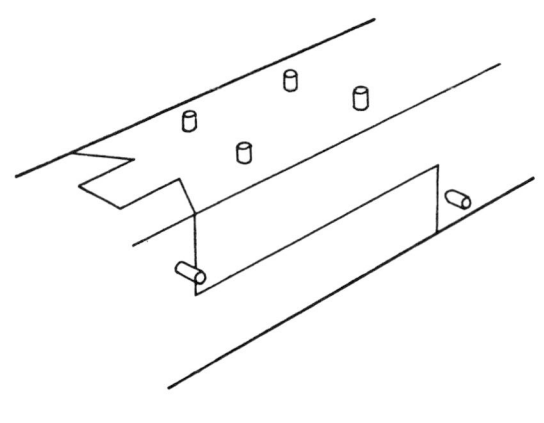

Diagram 228 *Edge-halved scarf with bird's-mouthed bridled butts, four face pegs and two edge pegs.*

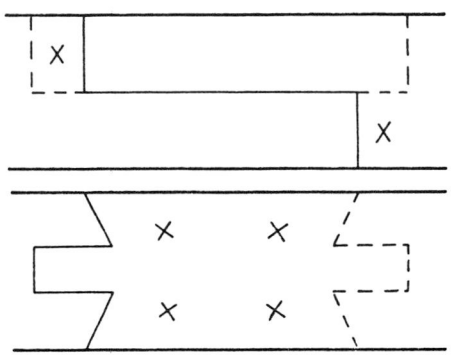

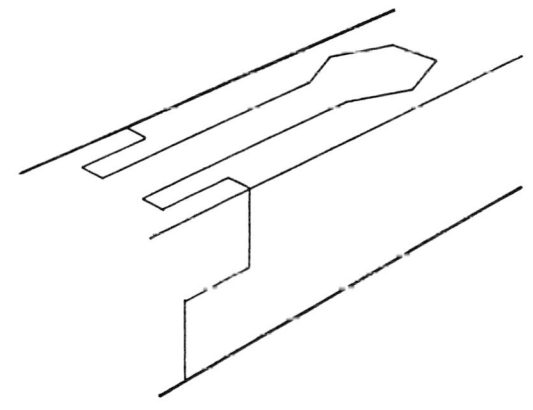

Diagram 229 Mechigai-koshikake-kama-tsugi *(lapped, gooseneck mortise and tenon joint with stub tenon).*

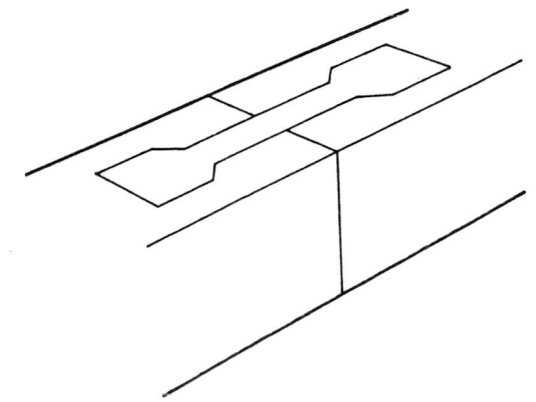

Diagram 230 Chigiri-tsugi *(inserted tenon joint).*

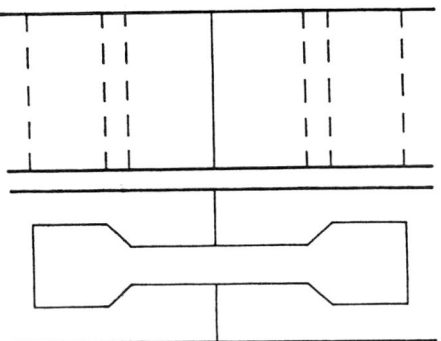

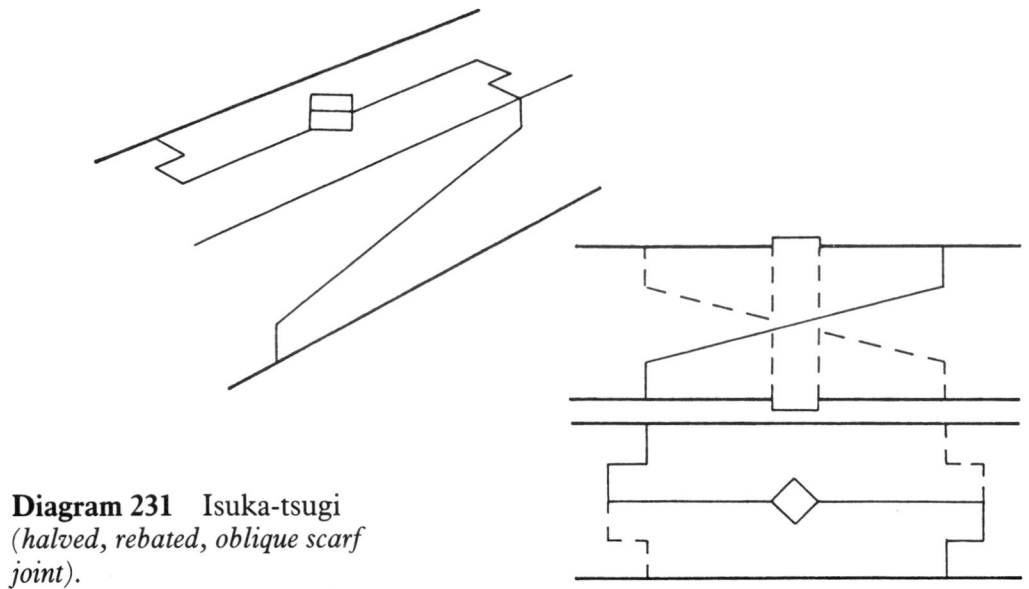

Diagram 231 Isuka-tsugi
(*halved, rebated, oblique scarf
joint*).

5 Miscellaneous Joints

Inevitably there are joints that do not come under any of the previous chapter headings, usually because they have been designed for specific, specialized situations.

JOINTS ALLOWING FOR EXPANSION AND CONTRACTION

Tenoned and mitred clamp

The problem of preventing warpage while allowing for expansion and contraction in a solid table top is usually overcome by using a tenoned and mitred clamp (*diagram 232*). This may not be ideal in every case because the mitre

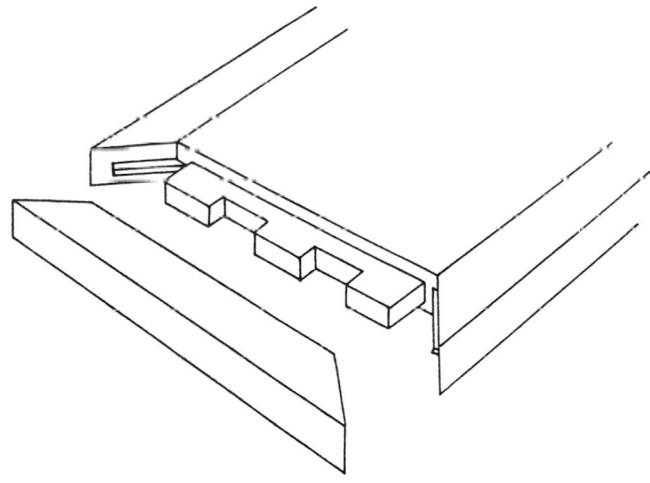

Diagram 232 *Tenoned and mitred clamp.*

will tend to open. The Greene brothers devised a method of overcoming this problem, using their familiar type of contrasting insert to create visual interest (*diagram 233* and *figure 35*).

When boards have been edge-jointed to make up the top, each end is planed square and a wide tenon formed. This

Diagram 233 *Alternative edge clamp devised by the Greene brothers.*

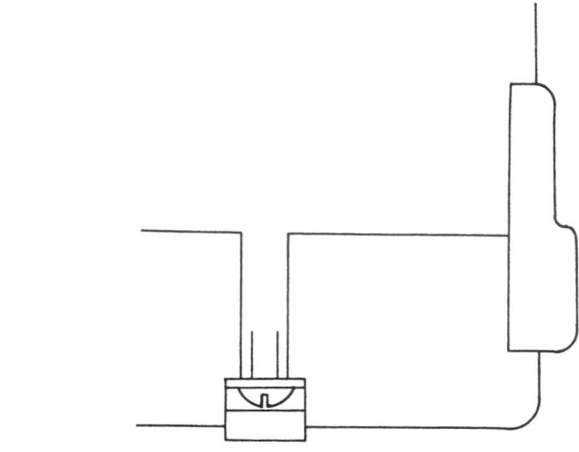

Figure 35 *Tenoned clamp with contrasting plugs.*

should be one-third the thickness of the boards with a length dependent on the size of top. A corresponding groove is cut into the clamp and placed in position (*diagram 234*).

On the outside edge of the clamp, a series of mortises are cut at regular intervals, depending on the width of board, to accept the round-headed screw and washer. This should

Diagram 234 *The wide tenon at the end of the board and the corresponding groove in the clamp.*

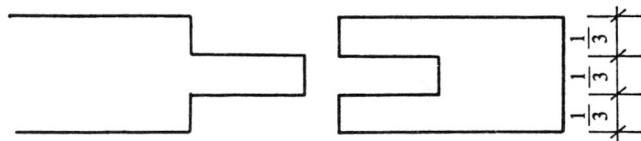

allow expansion and contraction to take place. The width of the through mortise is one-quarter of the clamp thickness, with the stopped mortise being as big again and symmetrical to it (*diagram 235*).

The clamp is left slightly longer than the width of the board, and a contrasting peg set into a mortise is used to cover the edge (*diagram 236*). This peg is glued into the main board but left dry on the clamp to allow for any necessary movement. Each mortise is plugged with the same type of contrasting material.

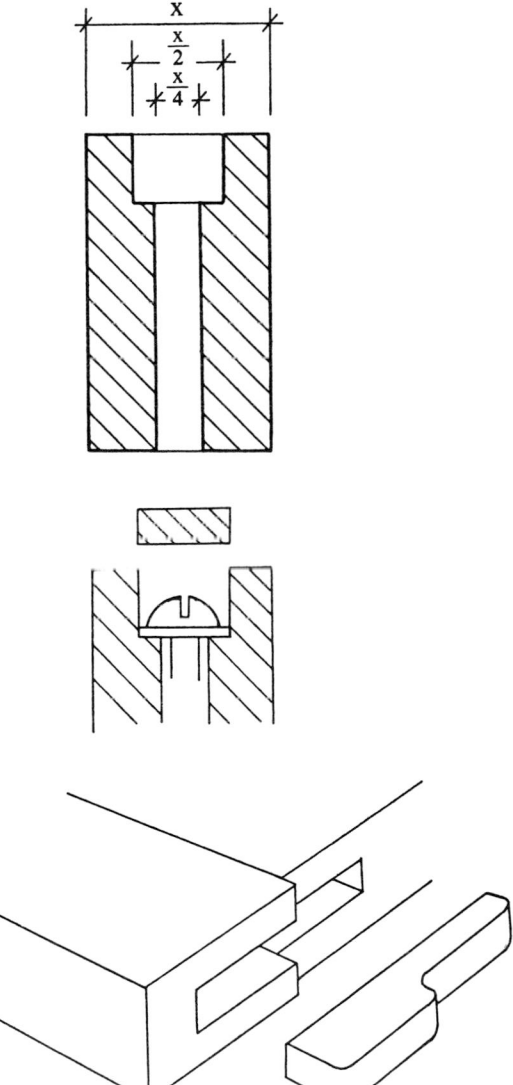

Diagram 235 *Sectional profile of the through and stopped mortises.*

Diagram 236 *Contrasting inserts are cut in the edge and end of the clamp.*

Mirror frame decorative joint

A similar type of joint used by the Greene brothers can be seen in a mirror frame and is more decorative than structural (*diagram 237* and *figure 36*). It is used in addition to a butt mortise and tenon, resisting any tendency to twist in the rail.

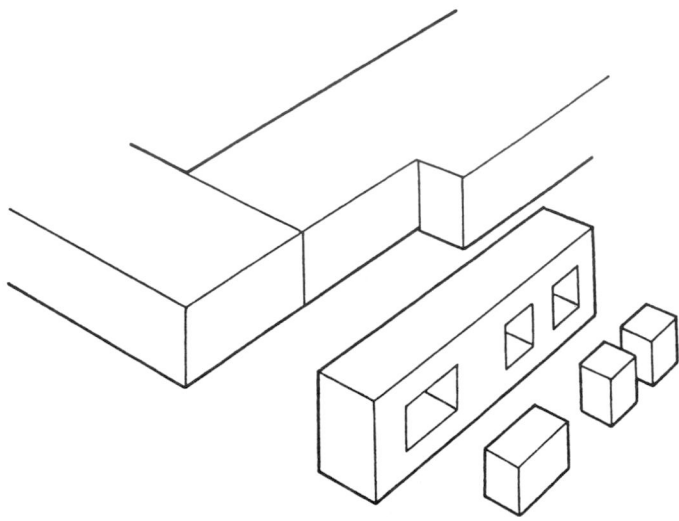

Diagram 237   *The decorative joint used in a mirror frame by the Greene brothers.*

Figure 36   *Decorative joint used in a mirror frame.*

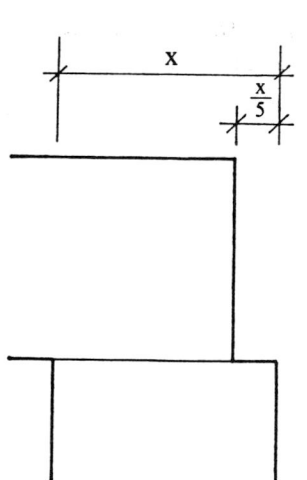

Diagram 238   *Proportions of adjacent rails.*

The frame is made in the same manner as a standard mortise and tenon frame, except that the length of tenon should be one-fifth the rail width. The overlapping rail is shorter than the outside dimension of the frame by two-fifths of its width (*diagram 238*). After gluing the frame together, extend the recess that accepts the contrasting slip into the adjoining rail (*diagram 239*).

To allow for expansion and contraction, the contrasting

slip should be glued and screwed to the side grain of one rail and slot screwed into the end grain of the other (*diagram 240*). All dimensions of the slip are made slightly larger than the recess and all protruding corners heavily rounded. The plugs that cover the screwheads can also be raised and rounded, if desired.

Diagram 239   *Sawcuts extend the recess.*

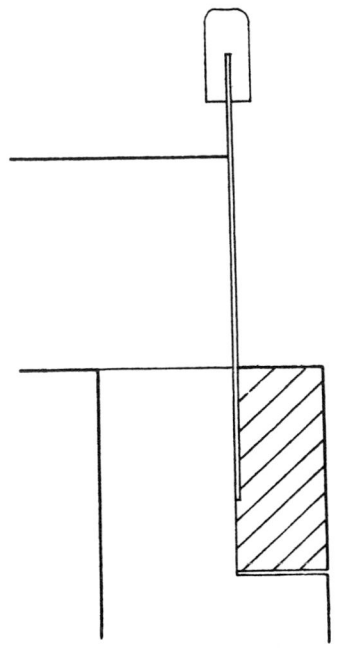

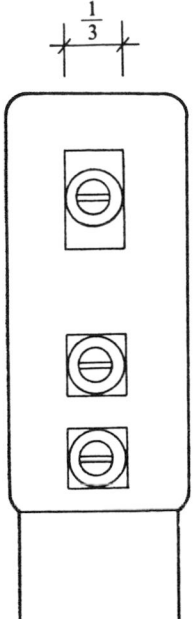

Diagram 240   *Position of each mortise that accepts the round-headed screw and washer.*

EDGE-JOINTING
Double dovetail (butterfly key) joint

If boards had to be edge jointed, the double dovetail or butterfly key was often used as a mechanical fastening to hold them together (*diagram 241* and *figure 37*). It is one of the oldest methods of construction, first developed for use in Egyptian boat-building.

Figure 37   *Double dovetail or butterfly key used when edge-jointing*

Diagram 241   *The double dovetail or butterfly key.*

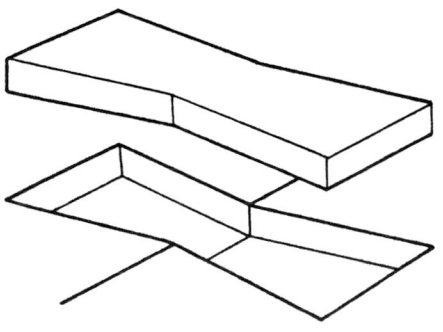

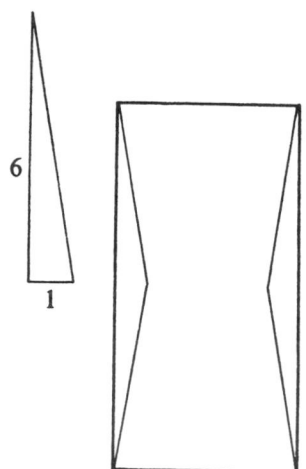

Diagram 242 *Profile of the key.*

A butterfly insert is cut with its grain running perpendicular to the boards, the length and width varying according to the size of boards being joined, and the maker's personal preference. Starting with a rectangular piece of timber approximately one-third the board's thickness, mark in the angles of the dovetail from the square end using a knife and sliding bevel (*diagram 242*). The waste is easily removed by sawing and trimming back to the lines with a paring chisel.

When the insert is complete, it is used as a template to mark out the recess with the internal 'V' lining up with the edge of the board (*diagram 243*). Sawcuts are made near the outline and across the width of waste which will assist timber removal (*diagram 244*). The recess is completed by removing the waste with the paring chisel and hand router.

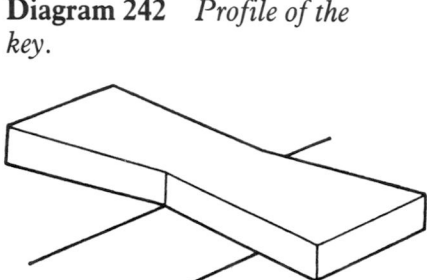

Diagram 243 *Using the key as a template.*

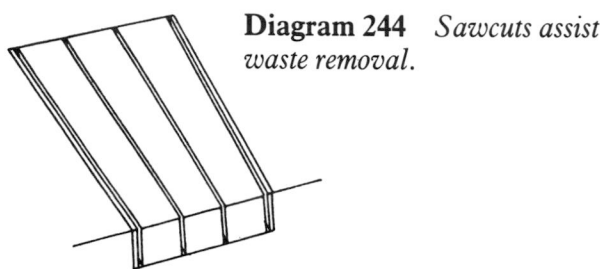

Diagram 244 *Sawcuts assist waste removal.*

When each key has been fitted into its respective recess, the boards can be assembled by applying glue to the edge and recess and cramping them together. Any protrusions should be planed flush after the glue has set.

Edge-jointing using contrasting dowel
An alternative method of employing a mechanical fastening when edge jointing boards uses a contrasting dowel to create visual interest (*diagram 245* and *figure 38*).

Diagram 245 *Edge joint using contrasting dowels and insert.*

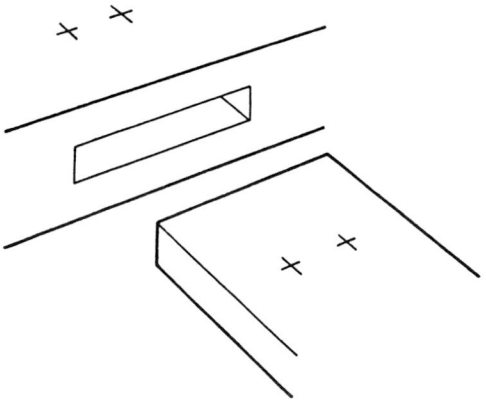

Figure 38 *Contrasting dowels used in the edge joint.*

A series of mortises are cut on the edge of the boards, their size and number depending on the maker's preference. A spline is cut that gives a hand-push fit with a length that is slightly shorter than the combined depth of matching mortises. The space that this creates at the bottom of each mortise will take up any excess glue.

The dowels are positioned symmetrically across the width of the mortise (*diagram 246*) with waste timber being used to prevent timber break-out as the holes are cut. One end of the slip can then be pushed into the mortise and holes drilled in it, using those in the board as a guide. The dowels can then be driven in temporarily while the boards are pushed together to locate the remaining centres on the tenon. These should be slightly offset so as to draw the boards together when constructed (*diagram 247*).

Alternatively, a gap can be left between the boards to create further interest (*diagram 248* and *figure 39*). The

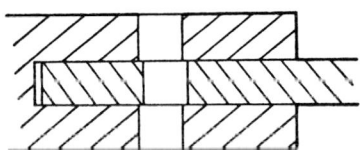

Diagram 246 *Position of dowels in relation to the insert.*

Diagram 247 *A staggered hole will draw the joint together as the dowel is driven in.*

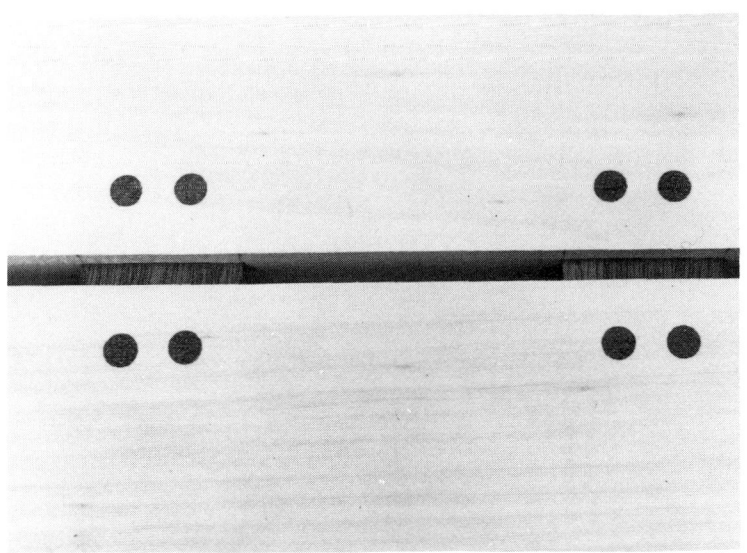

Figure 39 *Contrasting dowels and spline with a gap between the boards.*

Diagram 248 *An alternative edge joint to diagram 245 creates a gap between the boards.*

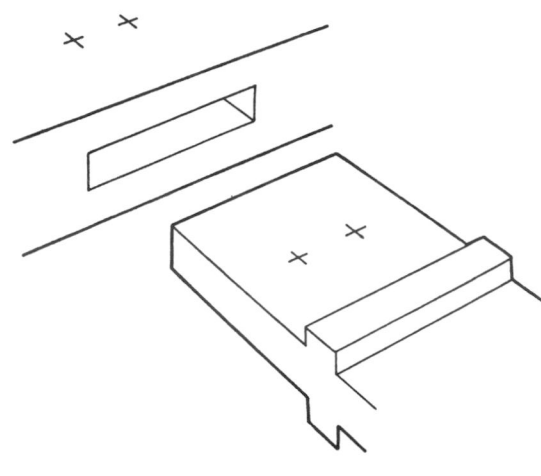

Diagram 249 *Proportions of contrasting insert.*

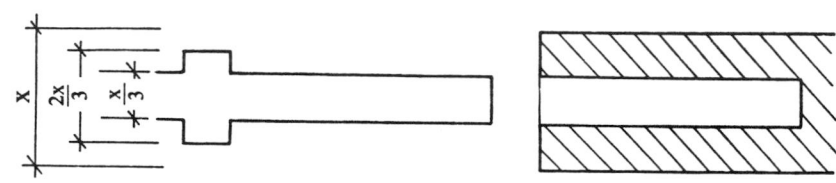

process of cutting is repeated with a shoulder being formed on the slip (*diagram 249*).

Shaker furniture

The search for perfection achieved in the simplistic forms of Shaker furniture is illustrated in the construction of the traditional oval box (*diagram 250* and *figure 40*). Visual interest centres around the joint which often varied in size depending on the box, but always used the same construction method.

Diagram 250 *The finger joint used in the traditional oval box produced by the Shakers.*

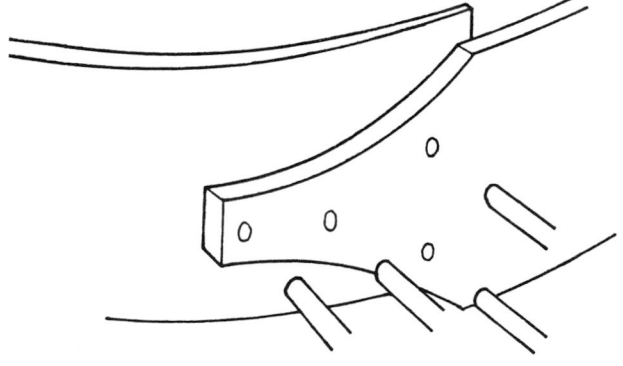

A broad band of timber (maple, cherry, etc.) usually about 3mm (⅛in.) thick was shaped at one end to form the fingers of the joint (*diagram 251*). A cardboard template should be made and used to mark in the outline on the timber. A coping saw is then used to remove most of the waste with trimming and chamfering done with the paring chisel. The opposite end of the timber is planed to a taper to prevent excessive thickness at the joint (*diagram 252*).

With all cutting done, the timber is steam bent around a pre-cut elliptical template. If more complex equipment is not available, simply hold the timber over the spout of a boiling kettle until the required flexibility is achieved. The projecting fingers can then be secured with copper rivets.

When the oval shape is set in position, discs of pine are fitted to create the top and bottom.

Figure 40 *Traditional oval box produced by the Shakers.*

Diagram 251 *Profile of the fingers.*

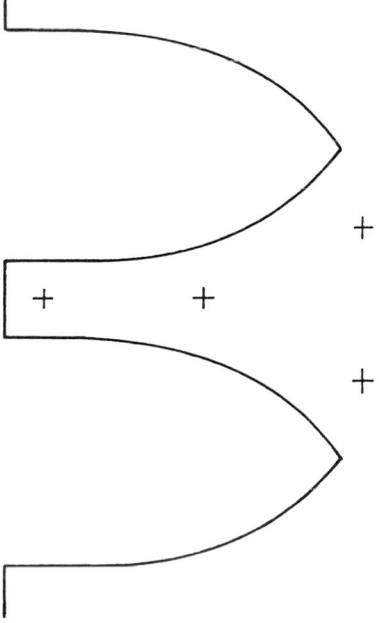

Diagram 252 *The opposite end of the strip of timber should be tapered to prevent thickness at the joint.*

Glossary

Bevel (sliding)   For measuring or marking any required angle

Boring   The process of cutting a cylindrical hole

Brace   A crank-shaped tool for holding and turning auger bits

Butt joint   Made by fastening together the ends or edges of two pieces of timber; the butt mitre uses two ends, each cut at 45°

C- or G-cramp   A fastening device shaped like the letter

Centre lines   Vertical or horizontal lines representing the centre of a symmetrical object

Chamfer   Bevelled edge or corner

Coping saw   A steel bow frame holding a narrow saw-blade

Groove   Channel or groove running with the grain

Housing   Channel or groove running across the grain

Jack plane   A general utility plane

Jig   A special device used for holding or guiding a tool

Kerf   The cut made by a saw

Laminate   To glue wood in layers; usually stronger than the original wood

Mortise   Usually a rectangular shaped hole cut into a piece of timber to accept another

Rebate or rabbet   Step-shaped reduction cut along timber's edge

Ryoba saw   Japanese-style saw that cuts on the pull

Sallying   To point or go forth

Smoothing plane   A short-soled plane used for final finishing

Splay   Divergent surface making oblique angle with another

Squinting   Oblique opening

Stickers   Thin strips of timber placed between boards to allow air to circulate

Taper   Narrowing gradually to one end

Template   A pattern or guide

Tenon   A projection cut on the end of a piece of timber which then fits into a mortise

Try-plane   Long-soled plane used for planing long square edges; a short version is called a fore-plane while the longer type is a jointer

Try-square   Used to check or mark a right angle

Veneer   Thin layer of timber

Vice   Used to secure timber while it is being worked

Tool Suppliers

U.K.

John Boddy Timber Co
Finewood and Tool Store
Riverside Sawmills
Valuation Lane
Boroughbridge
York YO5 9NJ

Buck and Ryan Ltd
101 Tottenham Court Road
London
W1P 0DY

Corbett Tools
224 Puxton Drive
Kidderminster
Worcs DY11 5DR

Curtis Holt Ltd
Green Street
Green Road
Dartford
Kent DA1 1FN

Gregory and Taylor Ltd
Worksop Road
Sheffield
Yorkshire

Isaac Lords Ltd
185 Desborough Road
High Wycombe

John Hall Tools Ltd
Clifton Down Shopping
   Centre
Whiteladies Road
Bristol

Record Ridgway Tools Ltd
Parkway Works
Sheffield S9 3BL

Sarjents Tools
44-52 Oxford Road
Reading RG1 7LH

U.S.A.

'Craftwoods'
York Road and
   Beaver Run Lane
Cockeysville
Maryland 21030

The Cutting Edge
1836 4th Street
Berkeley
California
and
7627 Miramar Road
Suite 3500
San Diego
California

The Fine Tool Shops Inc
28-28 Backus Avenue
Danbury
Connecticut 06810

Fox Maple Tools
The Snowville Road
W Brownfield
Maine 04010

Frog Tool Co Ltd
700 W Jackson Boulevard
Chicago
Illinois 60606

Garrett Wade Co
Dept 78
161 6th Avenue
New York
NY 10013

Greenlee Tool Co
2136 12th Street
Rockford
Illinois 61101

John Harra Wood and
   Supply Co
511 25th Street
New York
NY 10001

Leichtung Inc
4944 Commerce Parkway
Cleveland
Ohio 44128

The Toolroom
East Oxbow Road
Shelburne Falls
Mass 01370

Woodcraft
313 Montvale Avenue
Woburn
Mass 01888

Bibliography

Aaronson, Joseph, *The Encyclopaedia of Furniture*, Batsford, 1970

Ellsworth, Robert H., *Chinese Furniture*, Random House, 1974

Engel, Heinrich, *The Japanese House*, Charles E. Tuttle, 1964

Hewett, C.H., *The Development of Carpentry 1200-1700 (An Essex Study)*, David and Charles, 1973

Johnston, David, *The Craft of Furniture Making*, Batsford, 1979

Johnston, David, *The Wood Handbook for Craftsmen*, Batsford, 1983

Joyce, Ernest, *The Technique of Furniture Making*, Batsford, 1970

Makinson, Randell L., *Greene and Greene: Furniture and Related Designs*, Peregrine Smith Inc., 1979

Seike, Kiyosi, *The Art of Japanese Joinery*, Weatherill/Tankosha, 1970

Index